Everything That Matters in the Kitchen
Cook Book

by Dianne Linderman

Illustrated by Delores Uselman Johnson

ISBN: 1456319701
EAN-13: 9781456319700

Dianne@EverythingThatMattersRadio.com

www.EverythingThatMattersInCooking.com

Copyright 2010
Everything That Matters in the Kitchen Cookbook
First Edition, 2011

All rights reserved. No part of this book may be reproduced or utilized in any form or by any means, electronic or mechanical, including photocopying and recording, or by any information storage and retrieval system, without permission in writing from the publisher.

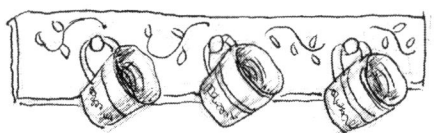

Dedicated to my children, Luke & Alexandra,
my husband, David, my Mom & Dad,
my 4 brothers and their wives,
my 17 nieces and nephews and grand nephew.

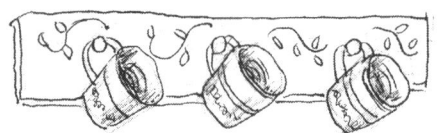

Contents

Soups 11

Salads & Salad Dressings 29

Breads, Crackers & More 43

Sandwiches, Empanadas & Wraps 55

Poultry 69

Seafood 89

Meats 99

Pasta, Eggs & Cheese 119

Side Dishes 129

Sweets 141

Beverages 167

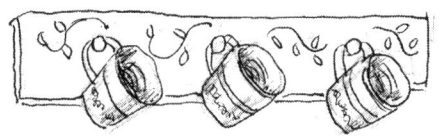

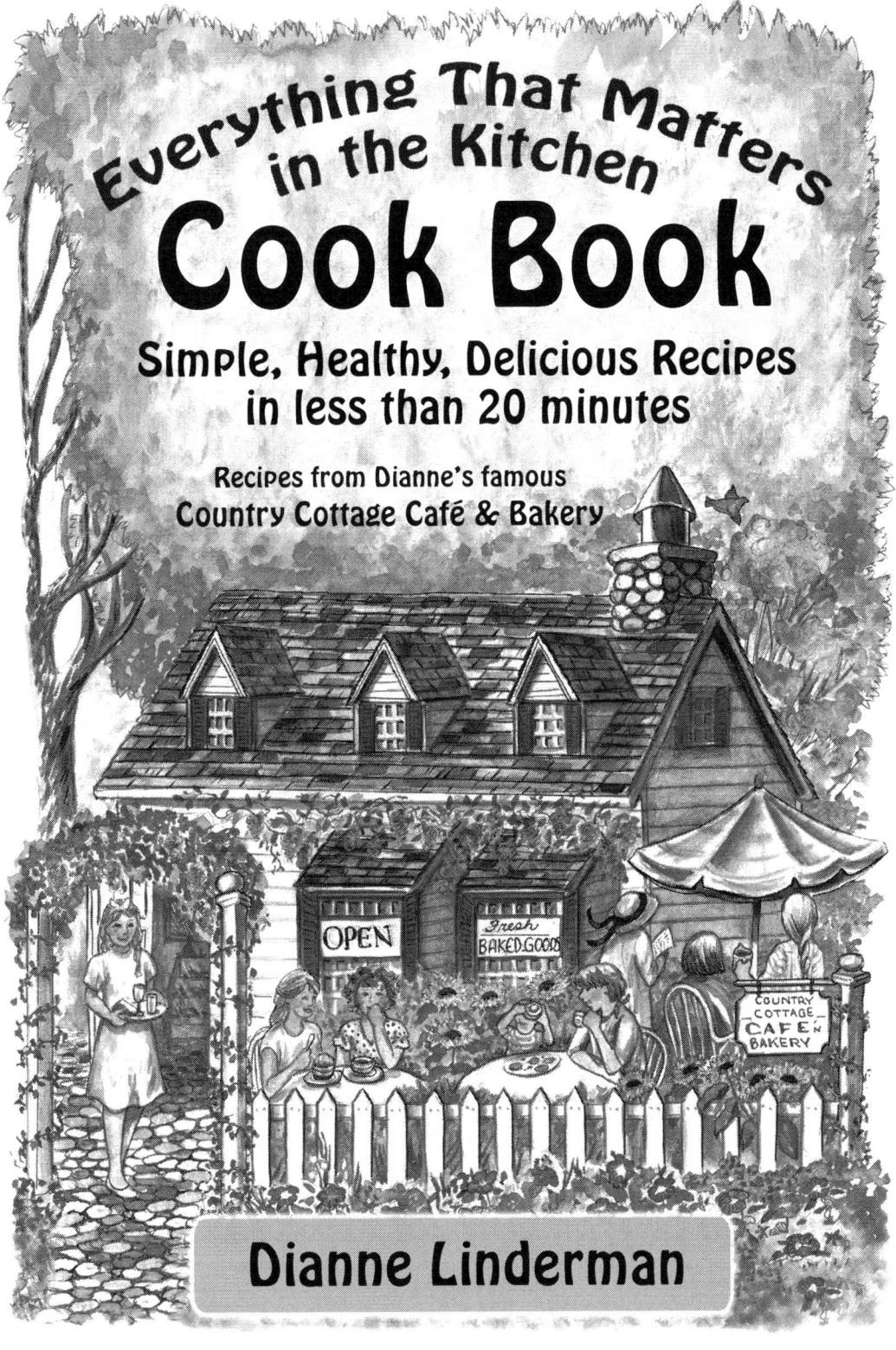

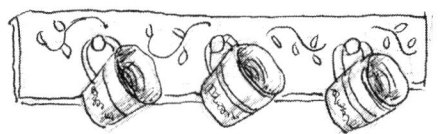

Soups

Asparagus Soup 12

Blended Veggie Soup 13

Cabbage and Mushroom Soup 14

Country Cottage Clam Chowder 15

Creamy Cauliflower Soup 16

Garden Corn Chowder 17

Hungarian Mushroom Soup 18

Light Cheddar & Butternut Squash Soup 19

Potato Soup 20

Real Jewish Chicken Noodle Soup 21

Salmon Chowder 22

Scallop Chowder 23

Simple Mushroom Soup 24

Split Pea Soup 25

Tomato Basil Soup 26

Asparagus Soup

2½ pounds **Asparagus**, trimmed and washed
4 tablespoons **Butter**
6 **Green Onions**, chopped
3 tablespoons **Oat Flour**
7 cups **Veggie Stock** or **Chicken Broth**
½ cup **Heavy Cream**
1 teaspoon **Grated Lemon Rind**
Salt & Pepper to taste

Break off asparagus ends and chop remaining tips into smaller pieces. Sauté green onions and asparagus in butter.

In a soup pot, add broth, asparagus and green onions. Boil on medium heat for approximately 35 minutes or until asparagus is soft. Stir in oat flour and then blend carefully in a blender or food processor. (Save a few pieces of asparagus for garnish on top of soup.) Pour blended soup back into pot and add rest of ingredients. Add salt and pepper to taste. Can be eaten warm or cold.

Blended Veggie Soup

Combine all of your favorite **Raw Vegetables** with either organic **Chicken Broth** or **Veggie Broth**, and blend them well in a food processer or blender. Flavor your soup with **Fresh Herbs** such as **Basil** or **Rosemary**. Add **Salt** and **Pepper** to taste.

This is a very healthy soup, so don't heat on high, just warm it or drink it cold. Yum!

Cabbage & Mushroom Soup

1 whole **Sweet Onion**, finely chopped
2 to 3 types of finely chopped **Cabbage**
1 whole bunch of fresh **Parsley**, finely chopped
3 **Garlic** cloves, minced
1 can **Tomato Sauce**
Garlic Salt & Pepper to taste
1 tablespoon **Honey**
Vegetable or **Chicken Broth** (enough to cover cabbage)
½ pound sliced **Mushrooms**

Place all ingredients, except mushrooms, in a soup pot and simmer until cabbage is soft.

Blend two-thirds of soup until puréed. Back on the stove, add mushrooms and warm until they are slightly cooked.

Country Cottage Clam Chowder

3 pounds **Red Potatoes**
26 ounces **Clam Juice**
½ **Red Onion**, minced
2 teaspoons **Garlic**, minced
½ bunch **Celery**, chopped
½ stick **Butter**
1 ½ teaspoons **Onion Powder**
1 ½ teaspoons **Garlic Powder**
1 teaspoon **Garlic Salt**
¼ cup **Oat Flour**
½ teaspoon **Black Pepper**
½ teaspoon **Dried Basil**
¼ teaspoon **Celery Salt**
1 ½ teaspoons **Dried Parsley**
½ cup **Chicken Broth** (powdered)
1/8 cup **Honey** (or more)
20 to 30 ounces of canned **Clams**
2 cups **Heavy Cream**

Peel and chop potatoes. Place in a soup pot and boil in clam juice until soft.

In a skillet over medium heat, melt butter and sauté the onion, garlic, and celery until transparent.

Add sautéed vegetables to the boiled potatoes and clam juice. Add seasonings, broth and honey. Bring to a simmer, for about 10 minutes, and then turn on lowest heat. In a bowl, mix 1 cup of the cream and all of the oat flour well. Add to the soup and simmer until thickened, stirring often. Add clams and rest of cream. Warm after adding cream, but don't boil.

Creamy Cauliflower Soup

2 **Cauliflower** heads, chopped
1 **Maui Sweet Onion**, chopped
2 stalks **Celery**, chopped
1 cup **Parsley**, minced
4 to 6 cups **Chicken Broth**, or enough to cover cauliflower
2 **Garlic Cloves**, minced
1 cup **Heavy Cream**
1 cup shredded **Cheddar Cheese**
Salt & Pepper to taste

In a large pot over medium heat, simmer cauliflower, onion, garlic, celery and parsley in chicken broth until soft.

Blend in a blender being careful not to put too much hot soup in the blender. You can blend half of the soup if you like chunky soup. Add the cream, cheese, salt, and pepper to taste.

Don't over heat the soup once cream and cheese are added. This is a delicious soup and will stick to your ribs. It is very low in carbs.

Garden Corn Chowder

1 tablespoon **Unsalted Butter**
½ **Maui Sweet Onion**, chopped
½ **Carrot**, chopped
¼ **Red Bell Pepper**, finely chopped
3 ears **Sweet Corn**, cut kernels from the cobs
3 medium **Red Potatoes**, chopped
3½ cups **Whole Milk**
Salt & Pepper
½ teaspoon fresh **Thyme**

Sauté the carrot, bell pepper and onion in butter over medium heat.

Combine all ingredients in a 4-quart soup pot and simmer for 30 minutes. Add salt and pepper to taste. If your corn chowder is too chunky, blend a portion of the soup in a blender. Be careful not to put too much soup into the blender, you can burn yourself.

Hungarian Mushroom Soup

4 tablespoons **Unsalted Butter**
2 cups **Onion**, chopped
1 **Garlic Clove**, chopped
1 pound fresh **Mushrooms**, sliced & washed
1 teaspoon dried **Dill Weed**
1 tablespoon **Paprika**
1 tablespoon **Soy Sauce**
2 cups **Chicken Broth**
1 cup **Milk** or **Cream**
3 tablespoons **Oat flour**
1 teaspoon **Salt**, or to taste
Ground **Black Pepper** to taste
¼ cup fresh **Parsley**, chopped
½ cup **Sour Cream**

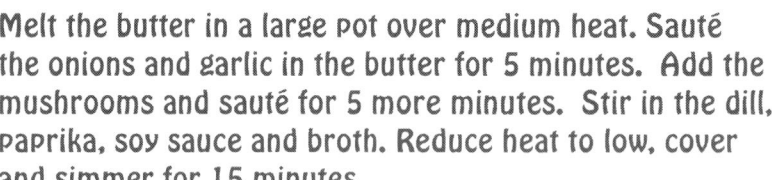

Melt the butter in a large pot over medium heat. Sauté the onions and garlic in the butter for 5 minutes. Add the mushrooms and sauté for 5 more minutes. Stir in the dill, paprika, soy sauce and broth. Reduce heat to low, cover and simmer for 15 minutes.

In a separate small bowl, whisk the milk and flour together. Pour this into the soup and stir well or you can blend in a blender to make a very smooth soup. Cover and simmer for 15 more minutes, stirring occasionally.

Finally, stir in the salt, ground black pepper, lemon juice, parsley and sour cream. Mix together and allow to heat through over low heat, about 3 to 5 minutes. Do not boil. Serve immediately.

Light Cheddar & Butternut Squash Soup

2 pounds **Butternut Squash**, peeled and cut into chunks
4 cups Organic **Chicken** or **Vegetable Broth**
1 cup **Sour Cream**, (you can use low fat, but I wouldn't)
½ cup **Light Cheddar Cheese**, grated
2 tablespoons **Salted Butter**
3 cloves **Garlic**, finely diced (optional)
¼ teaspoon **Ground Red Pepper** (cayenne)
1 tablespoon pure **Maple Syrup** (optional)
Several **Chives** for garnish, chopped

Combine the broth and squash in a large pot over medium heat and simmer until squash is tender. In a blender, carefully blend squash with broth until smooth. Return to pot and add the cheese and the rest of the ingredients. Warm up, but don't boil. Add salt to taste if needed. Garnish with chives.

Potato Soup

1 lb **Onions**, chopped
3 tablespoons **Unsalted Butter**
Heavy pinch **Kosher Salt**, plus additional for seasoning
5 peeled **Potatoes**, chopped
1 quart **Vegetable Broth** or **Chicken Broth**
1 cup **Heavy Cream**
1 cup **Buttermilk**
1/2 teaspoon **White Pepper**
1 tablespoon **Chives**, chopped
Optional—you can add **Cheese, Garlic, Bacon** and
   Sour Cream to make it a different type of potato soup.

In a 6-quart saucepan over medium heat, melt the butter. Add the onions and a heavy pinch of salt and sauté for 5 minutes.

Add the potatoes and the broth, increase the heat to medium-high, and bring to a boil. Reduce the heat to low, cover, and gently simmer until the potatoes are soft, approximately 45 minutes.

Turn off the heat and purée the mixture with an immersion blender or regular blender until smooth. Stir in the heavy cream, buttermilk, and white pepper. Taste and adjust seasoning if desired. Sprinkle with chives and serve immediately, or chill and serve cold.

Real Jewish Chicken Noodle Soup

In a large soup pot, combine the following ingredients:

1 large whole **Chicken**, rinsed
3 large **Carrots**, chopped
3 stalks **Celery**, chopped into large pieces
1 **Maui Sweet Onion**, chopped
1 whole bunch **Parsley**, finely chopped
2 cloves **Garlic**, minced (optional)
Salt & Pepper to taste
2 cups pre-cooked **Noodles** or **Rice** (brown rice is delicious!)

Add enough water to cover all ingredients. Cover pot with a lid and simmer over medium heat for approximately 1 hour and 15 minutes. Cook noodles or rice separately.

Allow to cool slightly. Skim soup of all visible fat, return to stove and warm on medium heat.

To serve:
Place noodles or rice and chicken pieces into individual bowls. Ladle hot soup over it and serve immediately.

This soup is great when you get a cold!

Salmon Chowder

2 tablespoons **Butter**
½ cup **Onion**, chopped
4 cloves **Garlic**, minced
2 stalks **Celery**, chopped
3 unpeeled **Red Potatoes**, chopped
4 tablespoons fresh **Parsley**, minced
7 ounces cooked **Salmon**, de-boned
Garlic Salt & Pepper to taste
1 ½ cups **Heavy Cream**
4 to 6 cups **Chicken Broth** or **Clam Juice**
2 tablespoons fresh or dried **Dill**, chopped
¼ cup **White Wine**
2 tablespooons **Honey** or **Maple Syrup**

Melt butter in a frying pan over medium heat. Add chopped onions, garlic, and celery and sauté them until translucent.

In large soup pot, place all ingredients except cream and honey. Add enough broth to just cover ingredients. Simmer until potatoes fall apart. Using a hand blender, or just a regular blender, purée ½ of the soup. Remove from heat and add cream. Taste the soup to see if adding a little honey could bring out the flavor.

Scallop Chowder

4 teaspoons **Butter**
Olive Oil Cooking Spray
1½ cups **Onion**, chopped
¼ cup **Celery**, chopped
3 teaspoons **Garlic**, minced
4½ cups **Red Potatoes**, unpeeled and chopped
1½ teaspoons **Garlic Salt**
1 teaspoon ground **Black Pepper**
1/1½ teaspoons fresh **Thyme**, chopped
6 cups **Clam Juice**
¼ cup **Oat Flour** for thickening
1½ cups **Milk**
1½ cups **Half & Half**
1½ pounds **Sea Scallops**, cut into 1-inch chunks
¼ cup fresh **Chives**, chopped

In a sauce pan, sauté onions, celery and garlic in butter over medium heat. Pour clam juice into a large soup pot and add all veggies, potatoes, herbs, spices, salt and pepper. Bring to a simmer and simmer until potatoes fall apart.

Add flour, stirring well with wisk, and continue to simmer until the soup begins to thicken. Now add everything else. Scallops cook very fast, and cream should not be boiled. This is as good as clam chowder.

Simple Mushroom Soup

2 to 3 pounds **Mushrooms** of choice, washed and sliced
1 **Leek**
1 tablespoon **Butter**
4 cups **Chicken Broth**
2 tablespoons **Oat Flour**
½ cup dry **White Wine**
3 tablespoons **Flat Leaf Parsley**, minced
Black Pepper
2/3 cup **Heavy Cream**

Cut leek in half and finely chop white and green parts. Place butter in a small saucepan and sauté leek over medium heat.

In a soup pot, add the rest of the ingredients, except the cream, and bring to a boil. Turn heat to low, and simmer for 15 minutes.

Blend half of the soup safely in a blender, add it to the remaining soup in the pot, and then stir in the cream.

Split Pea Soup

- 1 Ham Bone
- 1 pound dry Split Peas
- 4 cloves Garlic, minced
- 2 tablespoons each Butter and Olive Oil
- ½ pound Baby Carrots, chopped
- 1 whole Sweet Onion, minced
- Garlic Salt & Pepper to taste

Empty package of split peas into a colander or bowl, and sort through well, removing foreign matter and imperfect peas. Rinse well. Put peas into large soup pot along with ham bone and add enough water to cover peas.

In a frying pan, sauté the garlic, carrots and onion in butter and olive oil over medium heat. Add to soaking peas (add water if needed to just cover ingredients). Add garlic salt and pepper to taste. Simmer on low for about an hour, stirring occasionally—or bake in oven at 375° for 2 hours. (Baking in the oven keeps it from burning.)

Tomato Basil Soup

Our signature soup at the Country Cottage Café

6 to 8 large vine-ripened, organic **Tomatoes**
1 cup fresh **Basil**
1 cup **Whole Cream** or **Whole Milk** (optional)
2 cups **Chicken Broth**
3 to 4 cloves fresh **Garlic**, diced
Garlic Salt & Pepper to taste
1/8 cup **White Wine** (optional)
1 to 3 tablespoons **Maple Syrup**, unless tomatoes are really sweet
Tabasco or other hot sauce (if you like spicy soup)

Purée all ingredients in a blender. If you want chunky soup, blend half of the soup a little less. Warm, don't cook this soup for optimum health. If you like a richer soup, you can add 1/8 cup of white wine and simmer on low. Don't be afraid to experiment and add ingredients like Parmesan cheese. Garnish with some fresh basil.

Men, this soup is great for your prostate!

My Recipes...

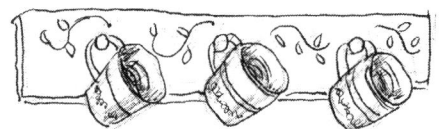

Salads & Salad Dressings

Cabbage Salad with Grilled Chicken 30

Ceasar Salad 31

Delicious Lemon Salad Dressing 32

Flax Oil & Balsamic Salad Dressing 33

Fresh Fruit Salad 34

Oriental Cole Slaw.. 35

Pasta Salad 36

Potato Salad... 37

Shredded Tex-Mex Layered Salad
  with Creamy Lime Dressing....................................... 38

Smokey Cabbage Slaw, Raw or Sautéed 39

Strawberry & Spinich Salad with Chicken 40

Cabbage Salad with Grilled Chicken

Boneless, skinless **Chicken Pieces**, chopped or cubed
1 cup **Teriyaki Sauce**
3 cloves **Garlic**, minced
Juice of 1 **Lime**
Garlic Salt & Pepper
3 different types of **Cabbage**
Any veggies...such as **Green Pepper, Soy Beans, Sprouts, Cilantro, Green Onion, Red Bell Pepper, Carrots, Peas**, etc.

Salad Dressing:
1 cup of **Seasoned Rice Balsamic Vinegar**
½ cup **Sesame Oil**
2 teaspoons **Garlic**, minced
Garlic Salt & Pepper to taste
2 tablespoons **Sesame Seeds** (optional)

Marinate chicken in the teriyaki sauce, minced garlic, lime, garlic salt and pepper. Cover and refrigerate for a few hours.

While the chicken is marinating, thinly chop up three different types of cabbage; Napa, curly leaf and red are my favorites. Add any veggies you wish and toss salad together.

Make the salad dressing.

Grill chicken on barbeque, oven grill or in a pan. I like to use dark meat, but you can use whatever you like. Toss the salad with the dressing and serve with chicken on top.

Ceasar Salad

Organic **Romaine Lettuce**

Salad Dressing:
¼ cup grated **Parmesan Cheese**
¼ cup **Water**
¼ cup **Fat Free or Olive Oil Mayonnaise**
2 tablespoons fresh **Lemon Juice**
½ teaspoon **Worcestershire Sauce**
½ teaspoon **Anchovy Paste**, optional
¼ teaspoon freshly ground **Black Pepper**
1/8 teaspoon **Dry Mustard**
2 to 4 cloves **Garlic**, minced

Whisk ingredients together and toss on rinsed and chopped romaine leaves. Add extra Parmesan cheese to taste.

Delicious Lemon Salad Dressing

2 Lemons (or more)
1/8 cup **Olive Oil** or **Grape Seed Oil**
Garlic Salt & Pepper to taste
Parmesan Cheese, optional

The only way to make this dressing perfect is to actually have your salad ready to toss. On a completely ready salad, squeeze lemons and add rest of ingredients. Taste your salad after you toss it and see if it needs more of any of the above ingredients. It always depends on the amount of salad you use—this recipe is for at least 6 cups of salad.

Flax Oil & Balsamic Salad Dressing

½ cup **Flax Oil**
Less than ½ cup of **Balsamic Vinegar**
Garlic Salt to taste
Parmesan Cheese (optional)

Mix all ingredients well. Pour over salad, and toss.

Fresh Fruit Salad

Cut up **Watermelon, Cantaloupe, Strawberries, Kiwi, Blueberries, Pineapple** and any other fruit you like. The flavors will blend and will be delicious.

Oriental Cole Slaw

4 to 8 cups of shredded **Cabbage**. I encourage you to use whatever type of cabbage you like—I like Napa cabbage.
6 **Green Onions**, chopped
1 tablespoon **Toasted Sesame Seeds**
½ cup **Toasted Almonds** (optional)
1 Cup **Ramen Noodles**, crushed
½ cup **Celery**, chopped
Grilled or cooked **Chicken Pieces**, sliced or chopped

Dressing:
1 tablespoon **Maple Syrup**
1 teaspoon **Garlic Salt** or to taste
½ teaspoon **Pepper** or to taste
1/8 cup **Seasoned Rice Vinegar**
1/8 cup **Sesame Oil**

For Dressing: Mix dressing ingredients in a small jar and store in refrigerator until ready to serve.

For Salad: Layer cabbage, celery, green onions and chicken. Add toasted sesame seeds, toasted almonds and ramen noodles just before adding dressing. Toss and serve immediately for best flavor and "crunch."

To toast almonds and sesame seeds, bake at 350° for 10 minutes in a single layer on a cookie sheet.

Pasta Salad

1 bag **Pasta Twists**, Barilla brand
1 bag **Veggie Twists**
1 whole **Maui Sweet Onion**, chopped
½ **Red Bell Pepper**, chopped
½ **Green Bell Pepper**, chopped
½ bag **Frozen Peas**
2 stalks **Celery**, chopped
12 ounce bag **Frozen Corn**
1 whole bunch **Parsley**, chopped
2 cups cooked **Ham**, diced
½ cup **Beets**, sliced

Cook pasta, following directions on bag. Cool pasta and place in large bowl. Add all ingredients to pasta and mix well with hands. Add dressing and then mix again.

Dressing:
2 packages **Italian Salad Dressing Mix**, follow directions using **Rice Vinegar** or **Balsamic Vinegar**
2 tablespoons **Teriyaki Sauce**
1 to 2 teaspoons of each **Celery Salt**, **Basil**, and **Honey**

Mix well in blender, taste, and add more spices as needed.

Potato Salad

4 pounds **Red Potatoes**, washed
1 whole **Maui Sweet Onion**, chopped
1 whole **Parsley** bunch, chopped
1 to 2 cups **Vegenaise** (egg-free mayonnaise)
4 stalks **Celery**, chopped
4 tablespoons **Mustard**
2 tablespoons **Celery Salt**
3 tablespoons **Salad Supreme Seasoning** (any brand)
2 tablespoons **Dried Basil**
Garlic Salt & Pepper

Boil potatoes until soft, but not mushy. Remove from heat and let stand for 15 minutes. You will notice that some of the skin has begun to peel away. Peel off the skin that comes off easily, and leave the rest of the skin on. Cool potatoes to room temperature.

Cut potatoes into cubes, place in a large bowl with the other ingredients, and mix well using your hands or a large spoon. Taste and add extra salt as needed. Refrigerate for 2 hours and devour!

Shredded Tex-Mex Layered Salad
with Creamy Lime Dressing

Salad:
Romaine Lettuce
Onion
Bell Peppers (red or green)
Black Beans
Cheese of choice
Shredded Chicken or Beef

Dressing:
2 tablespoons fresh Cilantro, chopped
1 tablespoon Red Wine Vinegar
1 teaspoon Lime Zest
¼ cup Lime Juice
½ cup Sour Cream (can use non-fat)
1 clove Garlic, smashed
1 tablespoon Honey
½ cup Extra Virgin Olive Oil or Flax Oil
Salt & Pepper to taste

Finely chop the lettuce, slice the onion and bell peppers and layer all ingredients. Make at least two to three layers. You may add anything you like to this salad; don't be afraid to try new ideas!

Blend Creamy Lime Dressing ingredients until smooth and refrigerate.

Drizzle dressing over salad and serve immediately.

Smokey Cabbage Slaw
Raw or Sautéed

1 slice of **Bacon**, cooked and chopped (optional)
½ **Onion**, chopped
½ cup **Red Bell Pepper**, diced
4 cups **Cabbage** and **Carrot**, shredded

Dressing:
½ cup **Seasoned Rice Wine Vinegar**
1/8 cup **Maple Syrup**
1 tablespoon **Grape Seed Oil**
2½ teaspoons **Dry Mustard**
1 teaspoon **Celery Seed**
Garlic Salt to taste

If you want to eat this slaw cold, mix well and devour. If you would like a warm dish, heat a frying pan or wok with 2 tablespoons of olive oil or grape seed oil, and throw in the bacon and the veggies. Sauté for about 3 to 5 minutes, then toss with dressing. Don't overcook this; it is much healthier if you undercook the veggies.

Strawberry & Spinach Salad with Chicken

2 bunches **Baby Spinach**, rinsed
4 cups sliced **Strawberries**
½ cup **Olive Oil**
¼ cup **Balsamic Vinegar**
¼ cup **Maple Syrup**
¼ teaspoon **Paprika**
2 tablespoons **Sesame Seeds**
1 tablespoon **Poppy Seeds**
2 cups **Chicken**, cooked and shredded
Garlic Salt to taste

In a large bowl, toss together the spinach and strawberries.

In a medium bowl, whisk together the oil, vinegar, syrup, paprika, sesame seeds, and poppy seeds. Pour over the spinach and strawberries, and toss to coat. You can also add chicken or shrimp.

My Recipes...

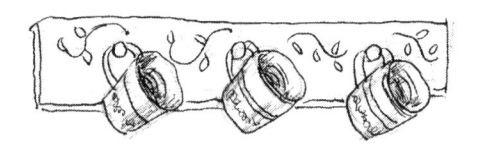

Breads, Crackers & More

Ancient Grain Bread 44

Farmhouse Crackers 45

Flaxseed Crackers 46

Focaccia Bread 47

Healthy Pizza Dough 48

Homemade Tortilla Chips 49

How to Make Butter 50

Ranch Bread 51

Ancient Grain Bread

1 cup **Sorghum Flour**
¼ cup **Brown Rice Flour**
¼ cup **White Rice Flour**
½ cup **Potato Starch**
¼ cup **Cornstarch**
¼ cup **Milled Golden Flax Seed**
2½ teaspoons **Xanthan Gum**
2 teaspoons **Active Dry Yeast**
1 teaspoon **Sea Salt**
2 **Eggs**
2 **Egg Whites**
1 cup **Water or Milk**
2 tablespoons **Vegetable Oil**

Combine all dry ingredients.

In a mixer, combine all wet ingredients.

With mixer on low, add the dry ingredient mix. Scrape the sides and mix on medium for 4 to 5 minutes.

Pour into a 9 x 5 pan and let rise to the top of the pan (roughly 75 to 90 minutes).

Bake at 350° for about 40 minutes. Remove from pan, cool & slice.

Farmhouse Crackers

Double up this batch.

1 cup **Whole Wheat Pastry Flour**
1 cup **Oat Flour**
½ teaspoon **Baking Powder**
½ teaspoon **Salt**
2 tablespoons chilled **Butter**, cut into small pieces
1/3 cup **Water**
1 tablespoon **Heavy Cream**

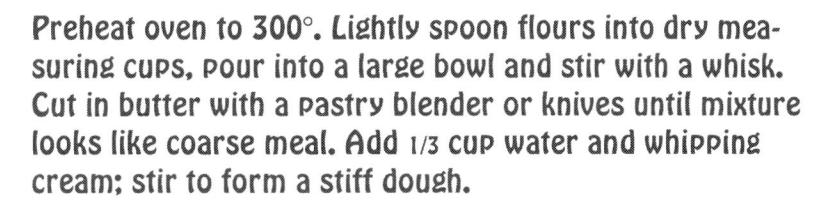

Preheat oven to 300°. Lightly spoon flours into dry measuring cups, pour into a large bowl and stir with a whisk. Cut in butter with a pastry blender or knives until mixture looks like coarse meal. Add 1/3 cup water and whipping cream; stir to form a stiff dough.

Roll dough into a 13-inch square on a baking sheet. Score dough into 16 equal squares. Pierce each cracker with a fork. Bake at 300° for 45 minutes or until crisp. Cool on pan. This recipe makes 16 crackers.

Flaxseed Crackers

1 cup **Flax Seed Meal**
1/3 cup **Parmesan Cheese**, grated
1 ½ teaspoon **Garlic Powder**
½ teaspoon **Salt**
½ cup **Water**

Heat oven to 400°.

Mix all ingredients together.

Spoon onto sheet pan, which is covered with a silicone mat or greased parchment paper.

Cover the mixture with a piece of parchment or waxed paper. Even out the mixture to about 1/8 inch. I find a straight edge, like a ruler, works well, although you can use a rolling pin or wine bottle too. The important thing is not to let it be too thin around the edges or that part will overcook before the center firms up. So after you spread it out, remove the paper and go around the edges with your finger and push the thin part inward to even it up.

Bake until the center is no longer soft, about 15-18 minutes. If it starts to get more than a little brown around the edges, remove from oven. Let cool completely—it will continue to crisp up.

Break into pieces.

The whole recipe is 6 grams of carbohydrate plus 35 grams of fiber.

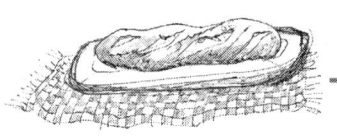

Focaccia Bread

Focaccia is one of the most popular types of flat bread available. It is an ancient bread that is a predecessor of the modern pizza and is often baked with herbs, cheese or other ingredients added to the dough.

1 package (¼ ounce) **Active Dry Yeast**
1 teaspoon **Maple Syrup**
1½ cups **Warm Water** (110° to 115°)
1½ cups **Oat Flour**
2¼ cups **Whole Wheat Flour**
¼ cup **Flaxseed Meal**
2 cloves **Garlic**, minced
¼ cup plus 1 tablespoon **Extra Virgin Olive Oil**
1 teaspoon **Sea Salt**
Rosemary, crushed

Place yeast and maple syrup in warm water. Let stand until it foams. In a large bowl, stir together the wheat and oat flours, flax meal, salt and garlic. Mix in the olive oil and yeast mixture.

When the dough has pulled together, turn it out onto a lightly floured surface, and knead until smooth and elastic. Lightly oil a large bowl, place the dough in the bowl, and turn to coat with oil. Cover with a damp cloth, and let rise in a warm place for 20 minutes.

Preheat oven to 450°. Punch dough down and place on greased baking sheet. Pat into a ½ inch thick rectangle. Brush top with olive oil and sprinkle with crushed rosemary. Bake 20 to 30 minutes or until golden brown. Serve warm.

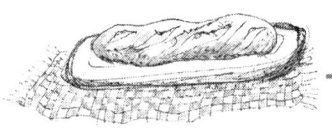

Healthy Pizza Dough

1 ½ teaspoons **Active Dry Yeast**
1 ¼ cups luke warm **Water**
1 teaspoon **Sugar** or **Maple Syrup**
3 teaspoons **Kosher Salt**
2 tablespoons **Extra-Virgin Olive Oil**
1 ¾ cups **Whole Wheat Pastry Flour**
1 ¾ cups **Oat Flour**

Place yeast in a bowl with ½ cup luke warm water and one teaspoon of sugar or maple syrup. Let yeast bloom for a few minutes.

In a bowl stir together 2 ½ cups of flour and the salt. Add the yeast mixture, oil and rest of the water. Mix with mixer or by hand very well. If you have a mixer with a dough hook, this would be the time to use it. Turn mixer on and add remaining ingredients slowly. Dough should be pliable and elastic. This takes about 10 minutes.

Shape dough into 4 balls. Place the balls on a lightly floured plate, cover with plastic wrap and let rest for 15 minutes.

Roll out and add yummy stuff!

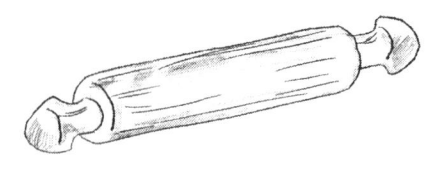

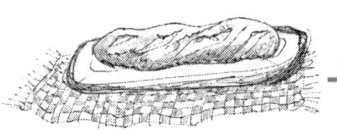

Homemade Tortilla Chips

1/4 cup **Olive Oil**
1 package **Corn Tortillas**
Salt, to taste

Stack and cut corn tortillas into wedges.

Heat olive oil in frying pan over medium-high heat and carefully place wedges into the hot oil. The tortilla wedges fry quickly, so watch that they don't burn. Lay hot corn chips on paper towels to drain, and sprinkle with salt.

Dip into homemade salsa—yum!

How to Make Butter

This is a fun thing to do with the kids...

Put as much **Heavy Cream** as you like in a jar with lid and shake (or use your blender) until solid (butter) separates from the liquid (whey).

Pour off whey through cheese cloth, then rinse off butter and add salt. Or, for my favorite, leave unsalted for sweet butter.

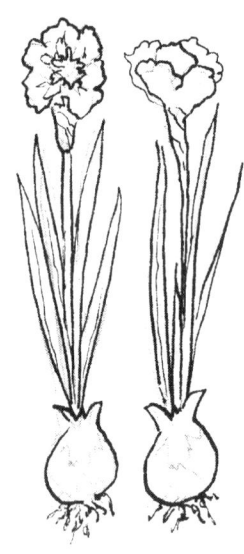

Ranch Bread

6 cups warm Water
¾ cup Molasses
¼ cup Dry Yeast
4 cups Whole Wheat Pastry Flour, or more
¾ cup Gluten Flour
3¼ cups Oat Flour
2 teaspoons Salt
½ cup Butter
½ cup Honey

Mix flours well. Oil six loaf pans. Combine warm water, molasses and yeast in a bowl and set aside until foamy, about 10 minutes.

Mix 3 cups of flour mixture, salt, butter and honey in a large mixer with a dough hook, and place these ingredients into a bowl and mix by hand.

Knead about 10 minutes, periodically adding more flour. Mix until the dough is no longer sticky. Place the kneaded dough into an oiled bowl and cover with a light towel. Set in a warm, draft free location to rise until double in size, approximately one hour.

Punch the dough down gently, using your fist, then divide into six equal parts. Shape into loaves, and place each in an oiled baking pan. Let rise again until almost double in size.

Preheat oven to 350°. Bake bread for 40 minutes. When done, remove bread from pans and cool on racks. Smother with butter and devour.

My Recipes...

My Recipes...

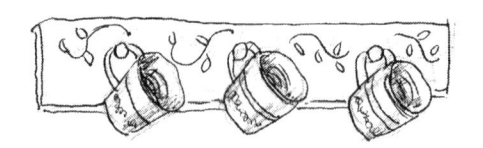

Sandwiches, Empanadas & Wraps

BBQ Tri-Tip Sandwich	56
Best Tuna Sandwich	57
Decadent Grilled Cheese Sandwich	58
Empanadas—Meat or Veggie Pie	59
Finger Sandwiches	61
Incredible Egg Salad Sandwich	61
South of the Border	62
Steak Wraps	63
The Ultimate Breakfast Burrito	64
Tomato Basil Baguette Sandwich	65
Turkey Peperoncini Sandwich	66

BBQ Tri-Tip Sandwich

3-5 pounds of good quality **Tri-Tip Beef**
Your favorite **BBQ Sauce**
Sourdough Rolls
Garlic Salt
Pepper

Cut tri-tip in strips and place in a crock pot. Add a medium size bottle of BBQ sauce, garlic salt, and pepper to taste. Turn crook pot on high for 6 hours, or slow cook for 8 hours. When it is done, pull apart the meat and place on big sourdough rolls.

Best Tuna Sandwich

What makes the best tuna sandwich?
#1 Quality **Bread**
#2 Quality **Mayonnaise** (such as grape seed oil mayo)
#3 Quality **Tuna** (in water)

2 cans **Tuna** (squeeze out water)
½ cup **Red Onion**, chopped
1/8 cup (or less) **Sweet Pickle Relish**
3 to 5 tablespoons **Mayonnaise** or **Vegenaise**
1 teaspoon **Yellow Mustard**
100% **Whole Wheat Bread**

Optional:
Apple, chopped
Toasted **Almonds**, chopped

Mix all ingredients well with fork, toast bread (optional), and spread tuna mixture on toasted bread. Add lettuce, sliced tomato and red onion to your sandwich.

Decadent Grilled Cheese Sandwich

Choose quality 100% organic **Whole Wheat Bread** or **Oat Bread.**

1. Lightly toast two slices of bread.

2. Spread small amount of quality **Mayonnaise** (try mayo made with olive oil or grape seed oil) on both slices of bread.

3. Choose any type of **Cheese** you like; my favorite cheese is white cheddar.

4. Add **Tomato** and **Basil** or whatever you would like.

5. Melt some love (**Butter**) in a pan on the lowest temperature.

6. Lay your sandwich into the melted butter and leave it alone until golden brown, then turn and brown the other side. You also want to make sure the cheese is melted.

Cut in half and eat with Dianne's Tomato Basil Soup.
Enjoy!!!

Empanadas—Meat or Veggie Pie

Dough:
3 cups **Flour** (plus a little more for kneading)
1 teaspoon **Salt**
½ cup **Cold Water**
1 **Egg**
1 **Egg White**
1 teaspoon **Vinegar**
3 tablespoons **Butter**

In a bowl, beat the water, egg, egg white and vinegar together. Set aside.

In a separate bowl, mix together the 3 cups of flour and salt.

Cut the butter into the flour mix with a pastry blender or two butter knives. Make a well in the center of the flour mix and pour the liquid ingredients from the first bowl into the center.

Mix the wet and dry ingredients with a fork until dough becomes stiff.

Turn the dough out onto a lightly floured surface. Knead it just until all the flour is incorporated and the dough is smooth.

Wrap the dough in plastic and refrigerate for at least 1 hour, but never more than 24 hours.

Prepare the work surface by lightly flouring the area where you plan to roll out the dough.   Continued...

Empanadas (cont.)

Roll out dough to about the size of a small flour tortilla.

Filling:
The fun with empanadas is that you can fill them with anything such as chili or tomatoes, basil and mozzarella cheese or left-overs like roast beef and mashed potatoes.

Here is one of my favorite combinations:
½ pound Ground Beef
½ Sweet Onion, chopped
Garlic Salt & Pepper to taste
Mashed Potatoes

Brown meat and onion in a large skillet. Drain fat then mix in mashed potatoes. Spoon ingredients into center of rolled dough. Fold over and pinch sides closed. Bake at 375° for 20 minutes or until brown.

You can also try the following combinations: Chicken with Swiss Cheese and Rice; Mozzarella Cheese, Marinara Sauce and Italian sausage; Onion, Shredded Beef, Peas and Mashed Potatoes. Be creative and have fun!

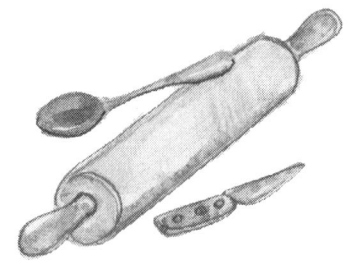

Finger Sandwiches

Two slices of **Whole Wheat Bread**, **Mayonnaise**, **Swiss Cheese**, sliced **Beef** or **Turkey**.

Cut off crust and slice into finger-sized sandwiches.

Incredible Egg Salad Sandwich

8 **Hard-boiled Eggs**, chopped well
¼ cup **Saffola Mayonnaise** or **Vegenaise**
1 tablespoon **Sweet Pickle Relish**
3 stalks **Celery**, finely chopped
1 whole **Sweet Onion**, finely chopped
2 teaspoons **Yellow Mustard**
Salt & **Pepper** to taste

Mix well and spread a thick layer on good quality sprouted wheat bread or your bread of choice.

South of the Border

This is a quick, low-carb lunch, dinner or snack!

1 large, low-carb, **Whole Grain Tortilla**
2 slices **Monterey Jack Cheese**
3 slices **Tomatoes**
Sprouts
Salt & Pepper

Place tortilla on a paper plate, lay cheese slices on top of tortilla and microwave until cheese is melted. (It's a good idea to lay a damp paper towel on top of tortilla to keep it moist.) Remove from microwave then add tomatoes, sprouts and salt and pepper to taste. You can add salsa or veggies, but this is so good you won't want to. Yum!

Steak Wraps

These are perfect to make when you have leftover meat, chicken, fish or even veggies.

Buy a package of **Large Wonton Wraps**. Shred **Steak, Chicken** or any combination of leftovers, and place a few tablespoons in the middle of each wrap. Fold them like napkins, using water to seal them.

On the stovetop, heat a skillet with an 1/8 inch of grape seed oil over medium heat. Place a few wraps in the oil, and brown them on both sides. Remove them from the oil and drain on a paper towel.

The Ultimate Breakfast Burrito

This is where you can get creative if you have left-over meat, chicken, fish or veggies. A low-carb tortilla makes a great breakfast, lunch, or dinner burrito.

Large low carb or **Whole Wheat Tortilla** or **Pita Bread**

Ideas for Breakfast Burrito:
Scrambled **Eggs**
Sautéed **Onion**
Sautéed **Spinach** or other **Veggies**
Any type of **Meat** or **Chicken**
Shredded **Cheese** of your choice
Black Beans (refried or whole)
Veggies

Ideas for Lunch or Dinner Burrito:
Chicken or **Beef**. You can use left-overs or a store-bought **Rotisserie Chicken**
Black Beans, (refried or whole)
Cilantro, organic
Tomatoes
Whole, Raw Cheese
Veggies
Salsa

Place tortilla on paper plate, add all of the ingredients, and fold like a burrito. Put a wet paper towel on top of the burrito to keep it most. Heat in oven at 300° or warm in microwave. Serve with salsa or be creative.

Tomato Basil Baguette Sandwich

Find a really fresh **Sourdough** or **French Baguette**, slice it down the middle and lay flat. Slice up some ripe **Tomatoes**. Pick some fresh **Basil** from your garden or buy some from a farmers market.

Here is a low-fat trick: Use Laughing Cow low-fat, low-cal **Cheese**, and spread generously on both sides of the bread. Lay tomato slices on one side of the bread and basil on the other. Drizzle tomato slices with **Balsamic Vinegar** and sprinkle with **Garlic Salt** and **Pepper** to taste. Yum Yum!!

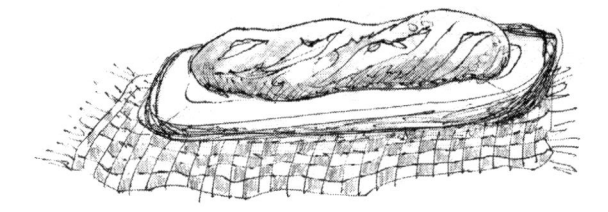

Turkey Peperoncini Sandwich

Our #1 most-ordered sandwich at the Country Cottage Café

Organic **Sourdough Bread**, sliced
Olive Oil Mayonnaise
Nitrate-free **Smoked Turkey**, sliced
Monterey Jack Cheese, sliced
Red Onion, sliced
Handful of **Peperoncinis**
Tomato, sliced
Ranch Dressing
Salt & Pepper

Toast bread until golden brown. Spread mayonnaise on both slices of bread. Place turkey on one slice of bread and place a slice of cheese, red onions and pepperoncinis on the other slice. Place both sides of sandwich under grill until cheese is melted. Add tomato slices, salt and pepper and ranch dressing. Cut in half and enjoy!

My Recipes...

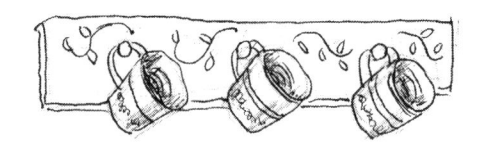

Poultry

Braised Chicken in White Wine 70
Chicken Parmesan 71
Chicken Pesto 72
Chicken Pot Pies 73
Chicken Scallopini with Mushrooms 74
Chicken Tarragon 75
Cornish Game Hens 76
Creamy Chicken Enchiladas 77
Curry Chicken 78
Delicious Italian Chicken 79
Dianne's Famous 10-minute Baked Chicken 80
Grilled Chicken & Garlic Pasta 81
Mushroom Chicken & Rice with Wine 82
Rosemary, Mushroom & Tomato Chicken 83
Rosemary Turkey with Stuffing 84
Salsa Lime Chicken 85
Teriyaki Chicken Fingers 86

Braised Chicken in White Wine

8 to 10 **Chicken Thighs** or **Chicken Breast**
1 cup **Dry White Wine**
Salt & Pepper to taste
4 **Garlic Cloves**, thinly sliced
¼ teaspoon **Thyme**
1 tablespoon **Butter**
3 tablespoons **Olive Oil**
Squeeze of **Lemon** or **Lime Juice**

In a large skillet, sauté chicken and garlic in olive oil and butter. Brown both sides then add wine, thyme and lemon juice. Cover and simmer turning once for approximately 30 minutes. As it reduces, liquid should thicken to a beautiful sauce. Serve with brown rice or mashed potatoes and a veggie.

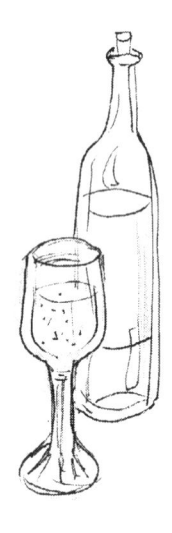

Chicken Parmesan

6 pieces of **Boneless, Skinless Chicken**, dark or white meat
½ cup **Oat Bran** or **Oat Flour**
Garlic Salt to taste
Pepper to taste
1 jar of **Newman's Basil Marinara Sauce**
1 box **"Barillia Plus" Angel Hair Pasta**
¼ cup **Grape Seed Oil**
¼ cup **Parmesan Cheese**

Prepare pasta and set aside.

Heat oil in a fry pan over medium heat. Dredge chicken in oat flour, sprinkle with garlic salt and pepper and place carefully into oil. Brown both sides, making sure chicken is cooked thoroughly.

Place a serving of pasta on a plate, place chicken on top and pour heated pasta sauce over both chicken and pasta. Sprinkle with parmesan cheese and devour.

Chicken Pesto

1 Whole (or 8 to 10 pieces) **Chicken**
1 jar quality **Pesto** (made with olive oil)
Garlic Salt to taste

Rinse chicken and pat dry with paper towel. Place in baking pan and sprinkle with garlic salt. Spread pesto all over chicken. Bake uncovered for 30 minutes at 500° or until lightly browned. Cover and bake for an additional 45 minutes.

Serve over brown rice or pasta.

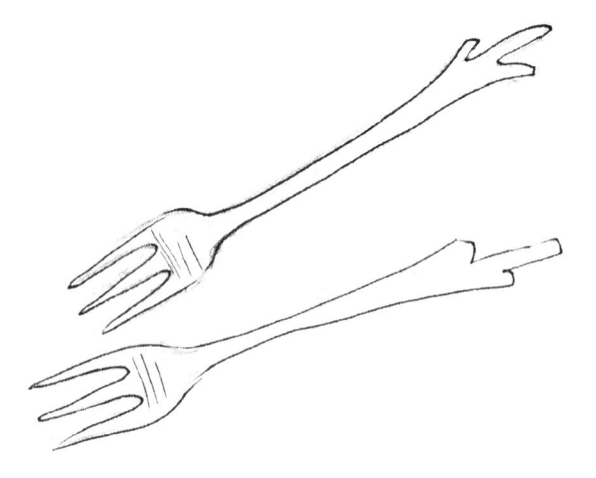

Chicken Pot Pies

2 whole **Chickens**
1 medium **Onion**, chopped
4 whole stalks **Celery**
1 bunch **Parsley**, chopped
5 **Carrots**, chopped
4 cloves fresh **Garlic**, finely chopped
½ cup **Oat Flour**
Garlic Salt & Pepper to taste
½ cup **Heavy Cream**
1 bag **Frozen Peas** (optional)
Pie Crust or **Croissant Pastry** (prepared Whole Wheat)

Wash chickens inside and out, and place in a soup pot with onion, celery, parsley and carrots. Add enough water to cover the chickens. Bring to a boil and cook for 1½ hours. Then let cool. Remove the chickens and celery stalks. De-bone the chickens and add the chicken meat and fresh garlic to the broth. Simmer for 10 minutes adding salt and pepper to taste.

In a separate bowl, mix cream and flour, stirring until all lumps are completely dissolved. Slowly add the flour and cream mixture and peas (optional) to the soup and stir well. Simmer for 10 to 15 minutes, stirring constantly, until the soup thickens.

Pour the soup mixture into oven-safe soup bowls or crocks and top with crust. Bake in a 375° oven for 10 to 15 minutes or just until the tops are light brown. Serve with a big green salad. (Instead of creating pies, you can also serve this mixture with dumplings.)

Chicken Scallopini with Mushrooms

6 **Chicken Breast Halves** or **Dark Meat**, boned and skinned
5 tablespoons **Unsalted Butter**
5 tablespoons **Olive Oil** or **Grape Seed Oil**
½ pound fresh **Mushrooms**, sliced
2 tablespoons **Green Onions**, chopped
¼ cup dry **White Wine**
1/3 cup organic **Chicken Broth**
½ cup **Heavy Cream**
Garlic Salt & **Pepper** to taste

Place chicken pieces between 2 sheets of waxed paper and pound with a mallet. Try to pound to a uniform thickness.

Heat 2 tablespoons each of the butter and oil in a sauté pan over medium heat. Add the mushrooms and sauté until tender, about 4 to 5 minutes. Remove mushrooms with slotted spoon and set aside.

Heat the remaining 3 tablespoons each of butter and oil over medium heat. Add the chicken and sauté, turning once, until browned, about 4 to 5 minutes total cooking time. Remove chicken and reserve.

Add the green onions to the pan and cook until tender, about 4 minutes, scraping the pan bottom with a wooden spoon to loosen browned bits. Add the white wine and chicken stock, bring to a boil, reduce heat to a simmer, and cook until the liquids are reduced by half. Stir in the cream and garlic salt and pepper to taste, add mushrooms and chicken and simmer to reheat. Serve immediately.

Chicken Tarragon

4 pounds Dark Chicken Meat pieces
2 tablespoons Garlic, minced
4 tablespoons Butter
1 Onion, chopped
Garlic Salt to taste
Pepper to taste
¼ cup Dry White Wine
½ cup fresh Tarragon
6-8 Mushrooms

Sauté chicken in butter, garlic and onion over medium heat. Sprinkle with garlic salt, pepper and white wine. Place chicken in a dutch oven with sauce from sauté pan. Add tarragon and cover. Bake at 400° for 45 minutes.

For an absolutely yummy addition, sauté sliced mushrooms in butter and pour over chicken.

Cornish Game Hens
with Brown Rice

4 or more **Cornish Game Hens**
2½ cups **Organic Chicken Broth**
Garlic Salt & Pepper to taste
¼ cup **Balsamic Vinegar**
3 tablespoons **Butter**, melted
1/8 cup **Maple Syrup**
4 cups **Instant Brown Rice**
Vegetable of your choice

Preheat oven to 400°.

Rinse hens inside and out, and pat dry. Spray bottom of baking dish with olive oil spray. Pour brown rice on bottom of pan. Arrange chickens on top of brown rice. Pour chicken broth over hens and brown rice. Place veggies around hens, and pour balsamic vinegar, maple syrup and melted butter over everything. Garlic salt and pepper everything well.

Bake without a cover until brown, then cover well and bake for approximately 45 minutes to 1 hour.

Creamy Chicken Enchiladas

2½ lbs **Boneless (dark or light) Chicken Meat**
10 cups fresh **Spinach**, torn and washed
1¼ cups **Green Onions**, finely chopped
3⅓ cups **Light Sour Cream**
1¼ cups **Plain Low Fat Yogurt**
½ cup plus 2 teaspoons **Oat Flour**
1¼ teaspoons **Salt**
2½ cups **Heavy Cream**
2 cups **Canned Green Chili Peppers**, drained
6 to 8 **Whole Wheat Flour Tortillas**
2½ cups **Jack** and **Cheddar Cheese**, shredded
Salsa for garnish

Bake, boil or grill chicken, then shred. Steam spinach and drain well. Combine chicken, spinach, cheese and green onions and set aside. In a large bowl, combine sour cream, yogurt, flour and salt. Stir in cream and chili peppers. Divide sauce in half and set one portion aside.

For filling, combine one portion of the sauce and the chicken spinach mixture. Divide filling among tortillas and roll them up. Lay each enchilada seam side down in a baking pan, spoon the second portion of sauce on top of enchiladas and bake in 350° oven until heated through. Sprinkle with cheese and serve with salsa.

Curry Chicken

2 tablespoons **Oat Flour**
6 Boneless, skinless **Chicken Breasts**
   (approx. 6 ounces each)
3 tablespoons **Olive Oil**
4 tablespoons **Butter**
1 **Sweet Onion**, finely chopped
2 **Garlic Cloves**, minced
2 to 3 teaspoons **Curry Powder** (medium to hot)
2 tablespoons **Frontier Chicken Broth Powder** or **Bouillon**
Garlic Salt & Pepper to taste
6 cups **Brown Rice**, cooked in **Chicken Broth**

Rinse chicken and pat dry. Flour chicken. In a large skillet over medium heat, fry chicken in half of the olive oil and butter until cooked. After slightly cooled, chop chicken and set aside.

In a skillet, melt butter over medium heat and then add oil. Sauté garlic and onion, then add rice, chicken and curry powder. As if you were cooking in a wok, stir rice and chicken with two wooden spoons. You can use the Frontier Chicken Broth Powder instead of salt, and if you need to, add more garlic salt and pepper to taste.

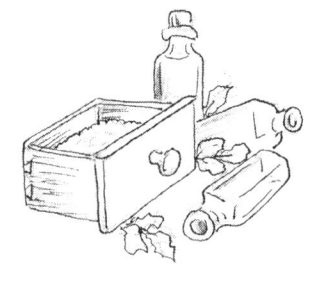

Delicious Italian Chicken

8 to 10 pieces of **Chicken** (I like to use dark meat)
3 tablespoons pure **Coconut Oil**
A jar of your favorite **Marinara Sauce**
¼ cup **Balsamic Vinegar**
Garlic Salt & Pepper to taste

Preheat oven 350°.

In a skillet over medium heat, melt coconut oil. Add raw chicken and brown both sides, then garlic salt and pepper both sides.

Place browned chicken in a baking dish and sprinkle with balsamic vinegar. Pour marinara sauce over chicken and cover with foil. Make sure foil does not touch pasta sauce. Place in oven for about 30 to 45 minutes. Check every once in a while to make sure the chicken is not getting too brown. Serve over pasta or mashed potatoes.

Dianne's Famous Baked Chicken
5-minute prep time!

1 whole (or 8 to 10 pieces) **Chicken**, rinsed and dried
¼ cup **Balsamic Vinegar**
2 pkgs of natural **Italian Salad Dressing Mix**
Garlic Salt
Potatoes & Carrots

Place chicken in a baking dish with potatoes and carrots. Pour balsamic vinegar over ingredients and sprinkle with Italian salad dressing mix and garlic salt.

Bake uncovered for 30 minutes at 500° or until lightly browned. Cover and bake for an additional 45 minutes.

Note: Check to make sure your oven is not too hot.

Grilled Chicken & Garlic Pasta

Marinade for grilling chicken or steak:
½ cup **White Wine**
½ cup **Balsamic Vinegar**
6 **Garlic Cloves**, minced
¼ cup **Olive Oil**
1 tablespoon **Honey**
Garlic Salt & Pepper to taste

Mix marinade and reserve half for pasta sauce.

Marinate pieces of boneless chicken 15 minutes before you grill. Spray oil on grill and when good and hot, lay chicken pieces on. After nicely BBQ'd, slice chicken in large pieces and serve over pasta.

Garlic Pasta:
10 **Cherry Tomatoes**, chopped
¼ cup fresh **Basil**, chopped
8 cups **Barrilla Plus Pasta** of your choice

Cook pasta and drain. Combine pasta, tomatoes, and basil with reserved marinade and toss.

Serve with green salad and veggies.

Mushroom Chicken & Rice with Wine

8 to 10 **Chicken** pieces
1 ½ cup **Chicken Broth**
½ cup **White Wine**
4 cups instant **Brown Rice**
3 tablespoon **Dried Basil**
1 pound **Mushrooms**, washed and sliced
3 tablespoons **Butter**
Garlic Salt & Pepper to taste

Preheat oven to 400°.

In a large skillet over medium heat, brown both sides of the chicken pieces in butter.

Coat a baking dish with olive oil spray, and spread the uncooked rice on the bottom. (Follow the directions on the box for the amount of rice. I use approximately 4 cups.)

Lay the browned chicken on top of the rice and drizzle with 1 ½ cups of chicken broth and ½ cup of white wine or cooking wine. Then sprinkle evenly with dried basil flakes, chopped mushrooms, and garlic salt and pepper to taste.

Bake in the oven uncovered for 10 to 15 minutes, then cover and bake for approximately 30 to 45 minutes depending on your oven.

Rosemary, Mushroom & Tomato Chicken

4 to 6 pounds boneless, skinless **Chicken**, cut into pieces
3 tablespoons **Butter**
3 **Garlic Cloves**
4 cups **Mushrooms**, sliced
½ cup **White Wine**
3 tablespoons **Fresh Rosemary**, chopped
1 can **Stewed Tomatoes**

In a large skillet over medium heat, sauté chicken and garlic in butter. Add mushrooms and sauté. Now add the rest of the ingredients, cover and simmer until chicken is cooked. Serve over angel hair pasta or brown rice.

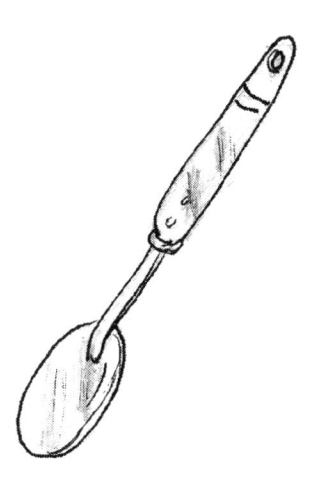

Rosemary Turkey with Stuffing

Purchase an organic or preservative-free turkey and clean thoroughly. Massage the skin with olive oil, rosemary, sage, garlic salt and pepper. Cut up apples and put into the cavity of the turkey. Place the turkey in large, oval Dutch oven and sear in a 500° oven until it is brown, approximately ½ hour. (If you have an electric oven, this may not work as well.)

Stuffing for 10 people:
Bake two pans of **Cornbread**
3 loaves of 100% **Whole Wheat Bread**
4 **Eggs**
2 whole **Onions**, chopped
3 stalks of **Celery**, chopped
1 to 2 bunches fresh **Parsley**
3 cloves **Garlic**, finely chopped
4 cups **Chicken Broth**
2 sticks of **Salted Butter**
Honey to sweeten it up if needed
2 teaspoons **Sage**
1 teaspoon **Thyme**
Poultry Seasoning, (a few teaspoons, optional)

In a large bowl, crumble bread and corn bread then add all of the ingredients and mix well. Taste the mixture, if it needs more salt or butter, you can add as needed.

After the turkey has been seared, fill every part of it. Bake covered at 500° basting every few hours. You will have to calculate how long it will take to roast your turkey depending on how heavy it is. If you bake it at 500°, it will take less time. This is my favorite stuffing ever!

Salsa Lime Chicken

1 Whole or 8 to 10 pieces **Chicken**
1 clove **Garlic**
Garlic Salt to taste
¼ cup **Lime Juice** (bottled or fresh)
2 cups fresh organic **Red Salsa**

Place chicken in baking pan and sprinkle with garlic salt. Cover with chopped garlic, lime juice and salsa.

Bake uncovered for 30 minutes at 500° or until lightly browned. Cover and bake for an additional 45 minutes.

Serve over barley, couscous, brown rice or vegetables and garnish with fresh salsa.

Teriyaki Chicken Fingers

6 pieces boneless, skinless **Chicken**
2 cups **Teriyaki Sauce**
1 cup **Whole Wheat Flour**
¼ cup **Olive Oil**

Rinse chicken and pat dry then cut into 1 to 2 inch thick strips. In a large plastic bag, pour 2 cups of your favorite teriyaki sauce and add chicken. Leave in refrigerator to marinate overnight.

The next day, roll chicken in flour until it is covered. In a frying pan over medium-high heat, heat ¼ cup olive oil and place floured chicken in it and fry until golden brown. Place on a paper towel to let drain. Eat hot or cold!

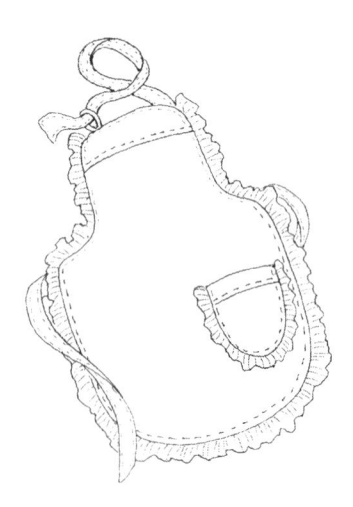

My Recipes...

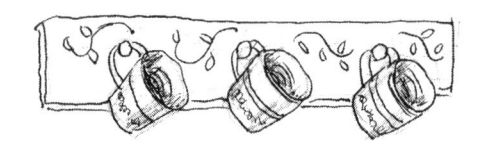

Seafood

Broiled Salmon 90

California Sushi Roll 91

Meals on a Grill 93

Salmon Cakes 94

Salmon Ceviche 95

Salmon Tacos... 96

Broiled Salmon

1 large Salmon Fillet
Mayonnaise
Garlic Salt & Pepper

or...
Melted Butter
Lemon

There are two simple ways to make this tasty dish:

1) Smother the fish with mayo, garlic salt and pepper. Broil or bake at 400° for about 8 minutes.

2) Cover the fish with 5 tablespoons of melted butter and sprinkle with garlic salt to taste. Then squeeze lemon all over it. Broil or bake just like above.

Serve with Steamed Asparagus and Rice Pilaf (this is one thing I like to use from a box—Near East is very good.)

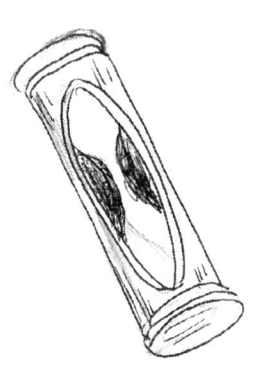

California Sushi Roll

1 cup **Rose Short Grain Sushi Rice** or **Brown Rice**
1 **Avocado**
1 **English Cucumber**
½ cup **Crab Meat** (real or imitation)
Mayonnaise to taste
½ tablespoon **Seasoned Gourmet Rice Vinegar**
Sushi Paper (nori seaweed)
Low Sodium Soy Sauce
Wasabi
Pickled Ginger

Rinse the sushi rice under running water until water is almost clear, and then cook with 1 cup of water in a rice cooker. If you don't own a rice cooker, simmer rice in a pot, covered, for 15 to 20 minutes or until done. You can use brown rice but it does not have the "stickiness" that is convenient for rolling the sushi—try a combination.

Place cooked rice in a bowl to cool. Add the vinegar and mix gently while fanning the rice to cool it. Set aside.

Peel the cucumber, then slice into long, thin strips. Also peel and slice the avocado into strips. Set aside.

Continued...

California Sushi Roll (cont.)

Put a seaweed sheet (nori) shiny-side down on a bamboo mat. Spoon rice on the nori sheet and spread to the edges, but leave about 1 inch at the furthest end from you.

Next, leaving about an inch on the edges of the spread rice, put a line of crab, cucumber and avocado across the rice.

Roll the mat beginning with the edge closest to you. Continue to roll until you reach the reserved inch you left at the furthest edge. Put some water across the reserved portion of the nori, and roll it completely over. The water will keep the nori edges together. Press down firmly on the edge to ensure a tight adhesion. Release the bamboo mat and pull it back towards you, leaving the sushi roll in place.

Dip a long, sharp knife in cold water to prevent it from sticking to the sushi rice. Slice the roll into small pieces. Make the second roll using the same method.

Serve immediately with soy sauce, wasabi and pickled ginger.

Meals on a Grill
Cook anything this way!

Fish fillets of your choice (salmon is best)
Large pieces of **Heavy Duty Aluminum Foil**
Garlic Salt
Butter
Teriyaki Sauce (optional)

Place butter and fish in the middle of the foil, then sprinkle with garlic salt. Form a packet rolling the sides tightly to prevent juices from leaking out. Place the foil packet directly on the fire or grill and cook for 10 minutes. Teriyaki sauce can also be dripped over the salmon.

Repeat the same steps for potatoes and also veggies.

Salmon Cakes

Approximately 4 pounds baked or poached **Salmon**
½ cup good quality **Mayonnaise or Vegenaise**
1/8 cup **Teriyaki Sauce with Ginger**
2 tablespoons **Dill Weed**
3 **Eggs**
2 teaspoons **Garlic Salt** (more or less)
½ cup **Oat Bran**
1/8 cup **Oat Flour**
¼ cup **Olive Oil**

Pull the bones from the salmon and shred into a bowl. Add the mayonnaise, teriyaki sauce with ginger, dill weed and eggs. Mix all ingredients well. Add garlic salt to taste.

Form patties, the size of a good size hamburger, patting the sides. Combine the oat bran, oat flour and garlic salt (to taste) in a bowl and dip the patties into the mixture.

Pour ¼ cup olive oil into a large skillet over medium heat. Add patties and brown one side. Turn only once. Brown second side and devour!

These delicious Salmon Cakes are even great cold.

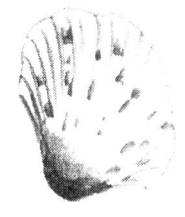

Salmon Ceviche

2 pounds **Salmon Fillets**, skinned and cut into ½ inch pieces
2 1/3 cups fresh **Lime Juice**
2 medium **Tomatoes**, seeded and diced
1 medium **Red Onion**, diced
½ cup **Olive Oil**
1 tablespoon **Cilantro**, chopped (to taste)
2 garlic **Cloves**, minced
½ teaspoon **Cumin**

Combine salmon and lime juice in a jar or bowl. Cover and refrigerate at least 30 minutes or up to all day, stirring occasionally. The salmon will become opaque, as the fresh citrus juice "cooks" it. Drain salmon well and combine with remaining ingredients.

Keep chilled before serving.

The absolute freshest salmon will produce the best flavor. This dish is very acidic, so it goes well with mildly flavored foods such as corn chips, avocados, potatoes, or freshly baked bread.

Salmon Tacos

2 pounds mild **Salmon**
2 cups **Red Cabbage**, shredded
¼ cup **Cilantro**, coarsely chopped
¼ cup plus 3 tablespoons red **Salsa**
Salt to taste
Package of **Corn Tortillas** (large)
Olive Oil for frying

Fry or bake the fish. Fry tortillas in olive oil. Place cooked fish into tortillas and top off with cabbage, cilantro, and salsa. Add tomatoes or whatever else you want.

My Recipes...

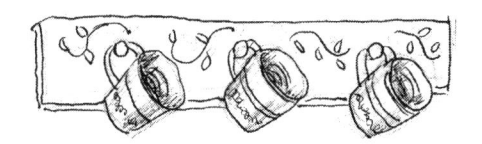

Meats

Autumn Farmhouse Stew 100

Balsamic Skirt Steak 101

Beef and Ale Stew with Dumplings 102

Braised Short Ribs 104

Cabbage Rolls 105

Corned Beef 107

Country-fried Steak (Healthy Chicken-fried Steak) 108

Cowboy Stew 109

Fried Wontons 110

Health Benefits of Lamb 111

Lamb Chops 112

Lamb Kabobs 113

Maple Balsamic Pork Chops 114

Pot Roast 115

Autumn Farmhouse Stew

This stew is full of root and cabbage veggies, very healthy!

1 whole **Chicken**
1 large **Onion**, chopped
2 to 4 **Carrots**, diced
1 whole stalk **Celery**
½ cup **Parsley**
4 ounces **Butter**
2 tablespoons **Oat Flour**
3 **Garlic** cloves, diced
1 small **Turnip**, cubed
½ **Green Cabbage**, cubed
1 cup of **Parsnips**, cubed
1 cup of **Tomatoes**, cubed
1/8 cup **White Wine** (optional)
Salt & Pepper
1 tablespoon dried **Basil**
2 to 4 tablespoons **Frontier Chicken Powder** (or other)
½ cup **Heavy Cream**
1 tablespoon fresh **Dill** for garnish

Place chicken into large stew pot over medium/low heat. Add all vegetables and seasonings along with enough water to barely cover chicken and veggies. In small saucepan, sauté garlic and add to stew. Cover pot and simmer on low for approximately 1½ hours. Check to see if chicken is done by pulling on leg. It should almost come apart; this is how you know your chicken is perfect! Take chicken out of the stew, allow to cool, and de-bone. Also take out celery stalk. Now add wine and simmer for 10 minutes. Taste and see if your stew needs a little garlic salt. You can now add cream or it may be perfect the way it is.

Balsamic Skirt Steak

2 **Skirt Steaks** (8 ounce)
¼ cup **Balsamic Vinegar**
4 cloves **Garlic**, minced
Garlic Salt & Pepper to taste

Smother a quality skirt steak with balsamic vinegar, garlic, garlic salt and pepper.

Marinate steak for ten minutes, and then place on a hot grill. Turn only once.

Beef & Ale Stew with Dumplings

4 to 6 pounds **Beef Shank**, cut into pieces
3 tablespoons **Oat Flour**
Salt & Pepper to taste
Olive Oil for browning beef
2 **Onions**, chopped
8 ounces **Mushrooms**, trimmed and quartered
3 large **Carrots**, peeled, halved and chopped
2 bottles **Ale** (12 ounces each)

Brown meat and pour into soup pot with all its pan juices.

Sauté onion and mushrooms in some of remaining meat juices then add them and all the remaining ingredients to the soup pot and turn the burner on low. Add both bottles of ale and simmer on low for 2 hours or put in a crockpot for 7 to 8 hours on low.

                                                Continued...

Dumplings (Cont.)

Make dumplings about 40 minutes before serving.

2 cups **Whole Wheat Pastry Flour**
¾ teaspoon **Salt**
½ teaspoon **Baking Soda**
½ cup **Green Onions**, minced
4½ tablespoons cool **Butter**, cut into small pieces
¾ cup **Buttermilk**
1 **Egg**

In a medium bowl, stir together flour, salt, baking soda and green onions. Using a pastry blender or your fingers, work cold butter into flour mixture until it resembles cornmeal with some pea-size pieces.

In another bowl whisk together buttermilk and egg. Gently fold wet ingredients into dry, mixing until a very crumbly dough forms. If more liquid is needed, add additional buttermilk 1 tablespoon at a time. Gently form dough into 12 equal balls and drop into stew.

Cover pot and cook 20 to 30 minutes. Let stand 15 minutes before serving. Stew will thicken as it cools.

Serve over mashed potatoes.

Braised Short Ribs

¼ cup **Oat Flour**
Salt & Pepper to taste
16 pieces bone-in beef **Short Ribs**
1/8 cup **Olive Oil**
Carrots cut into large chunks
2 quartered **Red Onions**
1 cup **Red Wine**
1 can **Chicken Broth**
Fresh **Thyme**
1 can **Chunky Tomato Sauce**

In a large skillet, heat olive oil over medium heat. Dip short ribs in flour and salt and pepper. Place ribs in hot oil and fry, turn only once. Brown both sides, add remaining ingredients, then cover and simmer over low heat for 20 minutes. (You can also cook in a crock pot.)

Serve with rice or mashed potatoes and veggies.

Cabbage Rolls

1 large head green or red **Cabbage** or **Kale**
1 pound ground **Bison Meat** or **Turkey**
1 cup **Brown Rice**
1 ½ cups **Chicken Broth**
¼ cup grated **Onion**
¼ cup grated **Red Pepper** (optional)
2 tablespoons chopped **Parsley**
1 **Egg**
¼ cup **Milk**
1 teaspoon **Garlic Salt**
¼ teaspoon **Pepper**

Sauce:
2 (8 ounce) cans **Chunky Tomato Sauce**
1 large **Onion**, sliced
2 tablespoons **Honey** or **Maple Sugar**
1 **Bay Leaf**
1 teaspoon **Salt**
1/8 teaspoon **Pepper**

Cook brown rice in chicken broth and set aside.

In a large pot, bring 3 quarts of water to boil. Add cabbage and simmer 2-3 minutes, or until leaves are pliable. Remove cabbage and drain.

Continued...

Cabbage Rolls (Cont.)

Carefully remove 16 large leaves from cabbage; trim center rib. If leaves are not soft enough to roll, return to boiling water for a minute.

In a large bowl, combine meat, rice, onion, parsley, red pepper, egg, milk, garlic salt and pepper. Mix well with a fork. (You can cook the meat in advance to allow for a quicker cooking time.) Add brown rice and mix.

Place ¼ cup of meat mixture in hollow of each of the 16 cabbage leaves. Roll sides of leaf over stuffing—rolling up from thick end of the leaf.

To make a delicious sauce, combine tomato sauce, sliced onion, honey, cloves, bay leaf, salt and pepper. Place in a blender and carefully blend.

Pour blended sauce into a large, heavy skillet. Arrange cabbage rolls, seam side down in a single layer in the sauce. Bring sauce to a boil over medium heat then reduce heat, cover and simmer for 1½ hours. Makes 6-8 servings.

Corned Beef

4 pounds lean, raw **Corned Beef Brisket**
3 tablespoons **Pickling Spice** (often included with brisket)
1 pound large **Carrots**, cut into 4-inch pieces
1¼ pounds large **Potatoes**
1 **Onion**, cut into wedges
½ head **Savoy Cabbage**, cut into wedges
½ head **Red Cabbage**, cut into wedges

Place the corned beef in a large slow cooker and scatter the pickling spices on top. Layer the carrots, potatoes and onion in the cooker (in this order for even cooking). Add enough hot water (4 to 5 cups) to cover the meat by at least 2 inches, put the lid on the slow cooker and cook on high for 4 to 5 hours. Add cabbage and cook for another 2 to 3 hours on low.

Country-fried Steak
(Healthy Chicken-fried steak)

4 **Cube Steaks**
½ cup **Whole Wheat Flour**
Garlic Salt & Pepper to taste
¼ cup **Olive Oil** for frying steak

Heat oil in frying pan. Flour steaks and then garlic salt & pepper both sides. Place steaks in frying pan and brown each side. You can tell the steaks are done when you see the juices seeping from the top.

Serve with mashed potatoes and a veggie.

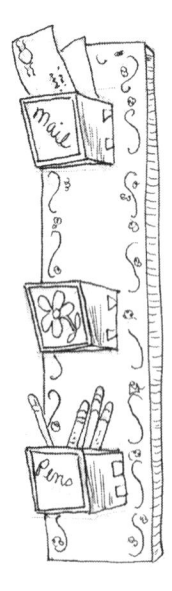

Cowboy Stew

3 to 4 pounds **Stew Meat**, cubed
3 pounds **Red Potatoes**, cubed
7 **Carrots**, chopped
1 **Yellow Onion**, chopped
2 tablespoons **Butter** for browning meat
2 stalks **Celery**, finely chopped
4 cloves **Garlic**, minced
1 large can **Crushed Tomato Sauce** with onions, celery, & garlic
2 cans **Amy's Tomato Bisque Soup**
2 tablespoons **Honey**
Garlic Salt & Pepper to taste
Can of **Beer** (optional)

Brown meat in butter over medium-high heat then combine all ingredients in large soup pot, cover and put into the oven overnight on 225° for approximately 7 to 8 hours. You may need to add ¼ cup water midway through. Don't be afraid to add more honey, salt and pepper. This should be a somewhat sweet and savory stew with a lot of sauce.

Fried Wontons

3 pounds low fat **Ground Beef** or **Turkey**
2 tablespoons **Garlic**, minced
½ **Sweet Onion**, shredded
¼ cup low sodium **Soy Sauce**
4 tablespoons good quality **Teriyaki Sauce**
Wonton Wrappers (large size)
Olive Oil

Mix meat well with hands.

Follow directions on wonton wrapper package for stuffing and folding. Fry in olive oil over medium-high heat until lightly browned and wontons are floating.

Drain and dip in low-sodium soy sauce.

Health Benefits of Lamb

• Lamb is a very good source of protein, with all 8 essential amino acids in the proper ratio. Four ounces of lamb provides 60.3% of an adult male's recommended daily allowance (RDA) of protein.

• Lamb is a good source of zinc, which is important for healthy immune function, wound healing, and normal cell division. Zinc also helps stabilize blood sugar levels and the body's metabolic rate, and is necessary for an optimal sense of smell and taste. Zinc is also important for maintaining prostate health. A four-ounce serving of lamb contains 38.3% of the RDA of zinc.

• Lamb is a good source of vitamin B12 which supports the formation of red blood cells and prevents anemia. It is also necessary for a healthy nervous system and the metabolism of carbohydrates, fats and proteins.

• Lamb is a good source of Vitamin B3 (niacin) which provides protection against Alzheimer's disease and other age related cognitive decline. Niacin is also necessary for healthy skin and the gastro-intestinal tract.

• Lamb contains very little marbling (internal fat throughout the meat) as compared to other meats.

• Lamb contains less saturated fat than other meat products; studies show that only about 36-percent of the fat in lamb is saturated. The rest is monounsaturated fat and polyunsaturated fat or the "good fat."

Lamb Chops

Coarse **Salt & Pepper**
3 tablespoons fresh **Lemon Juice**
1 tablespoon **Olive Oil**
4 fresh **Garlic Cloves**, minced

In a fry pan over medium heat, sauté the garlic in olive oil. Add lamb chops soon after you start sautéing garlic. Do not overcook your lamb; slightly pink meat assures its tender quality. Before the lamb chops finish cooking, squeeze lemon juice over them and sprinkle with salt and pepper.

Serve over pilaf or rice with vegetables.

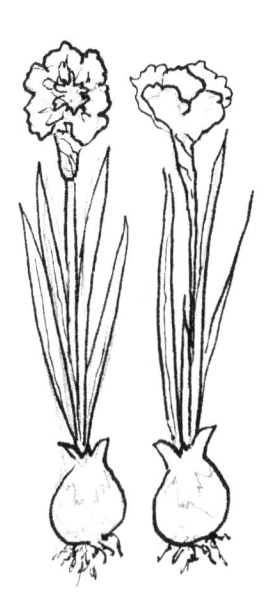

Lamb Kabobs

3-5 pounds **Lamb**
½ pound **Mushrooms**
10 **Cherry Tomatoes**
1 **Sweet Onion**, cubed
1 teaspoon **Garlic Salt**
2 cloves **Garlic**, minced

Marinade:
2 cloves **Garlic**, minced
1/8 cup **Dry Red Wine**
1/8 cup **Olive Oil**
1/8 cup **Orange Juice**

Cube lamb and marinate for 30 minutes. Place on skewers alternating the meat, onion, tomatoes and mushrooms. BBQ on hot grill for 15 minutes, turning about 3 times.

Serve in pita pockets or over rice.

Maple Balsamic Pork Chops

6 to 8 nice, lean **Pork Chops** or **Pork Steaks**
Oat Flour
Garlic Salt & Pepper to taste
4 tablespoons **Olive Oil**
4 tablespoons **Maple Syrup**
3 tablespoons **Balsamic Vinegar**

In a frying pan, heat olive oil over medium heat. Flour pork chops and sprinkle with garlic salt and pepper. Carefully lay pork chops in hot oil and brown both sides. Don't overcook. Drizzle with maple syrup and balsamic vinegar.

Serve with garlic mashed potatoes and vegetables. Also try a little fresh apple sauce on the side. (See page 147 for Fresh Apple Sauce.)

Pot Roast

1 jar of your favorite **Salsa**
6 **Garlic Cloves**, minced
4 to 6 pounds of high quality **Beef**
Garlic Salt & Pepper to taste
Red Potatoes, cut into large chunks
Carrots, chopped into large pieces

This is such a simple recipe!

Sear the meat in a frying pan over medium-high heat then place in a crock-pot with the potatoes, carrots, garlic and salsa. Turn crockpot on high for 1 hour and then on low for 6 to 7 hours.

Serve right from the pot or you may want to mash the potatoes you just made. Either way, this meal is absolutely delicious!

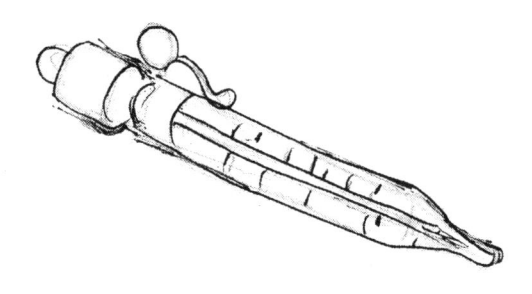

My Recipes...

My Recipes...

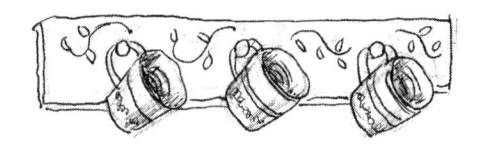

Pasta, Eggs & Cheese

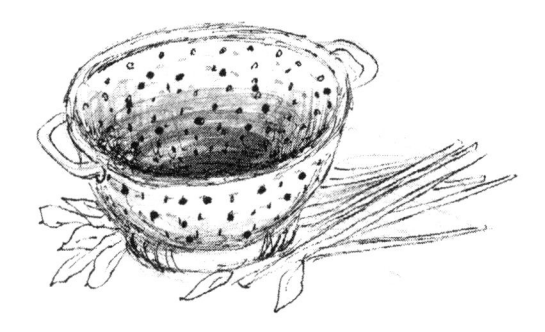

Dianne's Famous Quiche	120
Eggplant Parmesan	121
Mini Egg Muffins	122
Ricotta Cheese	123
Tomato Basil Pasta	124
Tortilla Pie	125

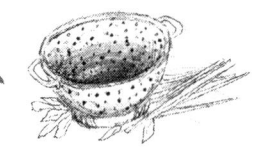

Dianne's Famous Quiche

½ cup **Heavy Cream**
4 **Eggs**, beaten
3 to 4 cups your choice of grated **Cheese**
Any kind of **Sautéed Veggies** you would like to add—my favorites are spinach, mushroom, and tomato
Salt & Pepper to taste
Prepared Whole Wheat Pastry Shell (optional)

Preheat oven to 400°.

Bake pastry shell in a pie dish for 10 minutes. Or, for a low-carb recipe, don't use a pastry shell; just spray olive oil spray onto a glass pie dish.

Add all veggies first, then add cheese. Cover with scrambled egg mixture leaving room at the top for the quiche to puff up. Bake for approximately 45 minutes to an hour. You can tell the quiche is done when it does not appear runny and does not jiggle.

Serve with a big green salad or use this as a breakfast entrée.

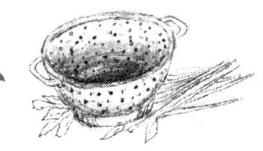

Eggplant Parmesan

1 to 2 large **Eggplants**, sliced 1/8 inch thick
1 to 2 pounds **Mozzarella Cheese**, grated
Newman's bottled **Marinara Sauce** (basil and garlic)
2 **Eggs**, beaten
Ground **Flax Seed** and/or **Oat Bran** for coating
Olive Oil for frying
Garlic Salt & Pepper to taste
½ cup **Parmesan Cheese**
Spray Olive Oil

Coat bottom and sides of a large lasagna baking dish with spray olive oil.

Dip eggplant in beaten egg then coat with ground flax seed/oat bran. Sprinkle with garlic salt. Brown both sides in frying pan.

Lay sliced eggplant on bottom of baking dish, and spread a nice layer of marinara sauce, 1/3 of the mozzarella cheese and 1/3 of the parmesan cheese over the eggplant. Sprinkle with a little garlic salt and pepper then add two more layers. Bake at 375° for approximately 45 to 55 minutes. Serve with a big green salad and garlic bread.

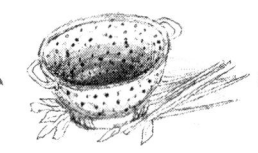

Mini Egg Muffins

6 Eggs
½ cup **Heavy Cream**
1 cup **Onion**, chopped
¾ cup **Low-Fat Cheese** (Laughing Cow Cheese)
Broccoli, or any other veggies or none at all
Sautéed **Onion**
Salt & **Pepper**
Tomato

This recipe is so easy! These mini quiche-type muffins are great for putting in your lunch or serving for breakfast, and you can add anything you like.

Preheat oven to 375°.

Spray each hole in a muffin pan with olive oil spray. Scramble eggs. Put veggies and cheese in each muffin tin first, now pour egg in and make sure you leave a little room for the mixture to puff up as it bakes. It is a little like a souffle as it will puff up and then shrink after you take it out of the oven. Bake for approximately 10 to 15 minutes. You can tell they are done by pressing your finger on them; they should feel firm.

Serve with some salsa. Yum!

Ricotta Cheese

1 gallon organic **Whole Milk**
2 cups organic **Heavy Cream**
¼ cup + 2 tablespoons organic **Distilled White Vinegar**
1 teaspoon **Kosher Salt**

Pour the cream and milk in a large, heavy-bottomed pot. Place mixture on medium heat and heat to just below the boiling point. Stir with a spatula to keep the liquid from scorching. Just before it boils, the surface will start to foam and release steam—about 185°.

Add the vinegar and stir for 30 seconds. The curds will form immediately. Add the salt and stir for another 30 seconds. Remove from heat, cover the pot with a dish towel and let curds stand at room temperature for 2 hours.

Line a colander with cheese cloth. Pour cooled mixture into the colander and drain for about 30 minutes. Gather the cheesecloth by its corners and twist until liquid is squeezed out. Remove the ricotta from the cheesecloth and store it in an airtight container in the refrigerator.

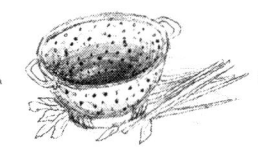

Tomato Basil Pasta

1 box Barilla PLUS Angel Hair Pasta (multi-grain pasta)
2 tablespoons Olive Oil
6 tablespoons fresh Garlic, chopped
4 or more cups organic Chicken Broth
4 cups fresh Tomatoes, diced and divided into two portions
3 cups packed Basil (divided into two bunches)
1½ cups Parmesan Cheese, grated (save some for topping)
Garlic Salt & Pepper to taste
¼ cup White Wine

Bring a large pot of lightly salted water to a boil. Add pasta, cook until al dente and drain.

In a separate pan, sauté garlic in oil over medium heat. Add chicken broth and simmer. Add half of the tomatoes, basil, Parmesan cheese, wine and sprinkle with garlic salt and pepper to taste. Simmer for ten minutes. Blend in blender or use hand blender directly in the pan. You can keep this a chunky sauce, or blend it until it is smooth. Spoon mixture over your plate of pasta and garnish with the remaining basil, tomatoes and Parmesan cheese. Serve immediately.

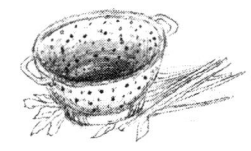

Tortilla Pie

3 Whole Wheat Tortillas

½ cup **Refried** or **Whole Black Beans** or any beans of your choice

¼ cup **Cheddar Cheese**, grated

¼ cup **Monterey Jack Cheese**, grated

Toppings: Chopped Tomatoes, Bell Pepper, Onion, Cilantro, Jalapenos, Olives, Avocado, Sour Cream and Salsa, or anything else you may want on your pie.

Preheat oven to 350°. Fry all three of the tortillas in oil over medium-high heat until crisp. On a cookie sheet, place one of the tortillas and cover with one third of any ingredients that can be heated such as the beans, cheese, and salsa. You may also want to add cooked chicken or beef. Cover with a tortilla and repeat the layer 2 more times.

Bake until cheese is melted, then garnish with all of the vegetables and cut into pie-shaped wedges.

My Recipes...

My Recipes...

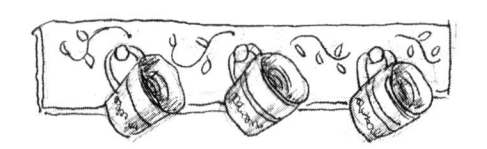

Side Dishes

Delicious Pinto Beans 130

Grilled Veggies 131

Homemade Tortilla Chips & Salsa 132

Homemade Mashed Potatoes.................................... 133

Rosemary Baked Potatoes 134

Sautéed Zucchini, Yellow Squash & Onions 135

Stir Fry (Base) 136

Stir Fried Brown Rice... 137

Delicious Pinto Beans

6¼ cups **Water**
1 cup condensed **Chicken Broth**
2 pounds dried **Pinto Beans**
5 cloves **Garlic**, chopped
½ **Red Onion**, chopped
5 tablespoons **Salt**, or to taste
2 tablespoons ground **Black Pepper**, or to taste
1 tablespoon **Red Pepper Flakes**, or to taste (optional)
1, 8-ounce package shredded **Mozzarella Cheese** (optional)
1, 16-ounce container **Pico de Gallo** (optional)
Add any other **Chopped Veggies** to top this off

Combine water, condensed chicken broth, beans, garlic, onion, salt, pepper, and crushed red pepper flakes in a large saucepan. Cover and bring to a simmer. Cook, stirring occasionally, until beans are soft (about 3½ hours). You may need to add additional water to keep the beans from drying out.

Mash cooked beans with a potato masher to desired consistency. Top with mozzarella and pico de gallo before serving. Now you can use these for tacos or for any recipe that you might use canned beans in!

Grilled Veggies

2 **Bell Peppers** (a variety of red, orange, or green)
8 large **Mushrooms**
1 whole **Maui Sweet Onion**
1 **Zucchini**
1/8 cup **Balsamic Vinegar**
1/8 cup **Olive Oil**
Garlic Salt & **Pepper**

Slice all vegetables in 1/16 inch slices. In a bowl, combine balsamic vinegar, olive oil, salt and pepper. Place all veggies into bowl and coat with marinade. Get your grill very hot, and, with a pair of tongs, place veggies onto hot grill. Sometimes it is a good idea to rub some olive oil onto grill to keep veggies from sticking. Turn only once and don't over cook. These veggies are great if they are still slightly crunchy.

Homemade Tortilla Chips & Salsa

1 package of **Corn Tortillas**
1/3 cup **Olive Oil**
Garlic Salt
Your favorite cookie cutter

You don't have to use the cookie cutter to shape the corn chips, but they are so cute. I like my apple cookie cutter. On a flat surface, place two tortillas. Cut as many chips out of the tortillas as possible. In a fry pan, add oil and heat until just before oil begins to smoke. Add a few chips, and cook on both sides until crispy. Drain on paper towel and salt lightly. Yum!

Homemade Salsa

1 pound fresh **Tomatoes**, (you can use canned tomatoes if you must)
½ cup **Sweet Onion**, chopped
¼ cup **Green Onion**, chopped
1 **Jalapeño Pepper**, seeded, (you can also use a milder pepper)
Squeeze 2 to 3 **Limes**
1 tablespoon fresh **Cilantro**, minced
1 clove **Garlic**, peeled
¼ teaspoon **Salt**

In a food processor, combine all ingredients; cover and process until chunky. Transfer to a small bowl.
When cutting or seeding hot peppers, use rubber or plastic gloves to protect your hands. Avoid touching your face.

Homemade Mashed Potatoes

4 pounds of **Red Potatoes** (leave skins on), washed & cubed
1 cup non-fat **Sour Cream**
½ cup real **Butter**
Salt & Pepper

Place potato cubes in a pot, cover with water and boil until soft, but not falling apart. Drain potatoes, add sour cream and butter and mash well. Be careful not to over mash because red potatoes contain a lot of gluten and will become sticky. Add salt and pepper to taste. Yum!

Rosemary Baked Potatoes

6 **Red Potatoes**
3 tablespoons fresh **Rosemary**, finely chopped
Garlic Salt & Pepper to taste
Spray Olive Oil

Heat oven to 375°.

Wash and dry potatoes. Cut them in half and in half again and then cut to make cube-sized pieces. Line a baking pan with foil and spray with olive oil spray. Place all potato cubes on foil and lightly spray them, then sprinkle with rosemary, garlic salt and pepper.

Bake in oven until top side is brown. With spatula, turn potatoes to brown the other side.

Sautéed Zucchini, Yellow Squash & Onions

2 to 3 **Zucchinis**
2 **Yellow Squash**
½ **Sweet Onion**
½ cup **Oat Flour**
2 tablespoons **Butter**
3 tablespoons **Olive Oil**
Garlic Salt & **Pepper**

Slice the zucchinis, yellow squash and sweet onion. Place in a bowl with the oat flour and toss. Heat the butter and olive oil in a skillet over medium heat. Add squash mixture and sauté until lightly browned. Add garlic salt and pepper to taste. This is one of my mom's Southern dishes.

Stir-Fry (Base)

6 cups cooked **Brown Rice**, (you can use quick brown rice)
1 whole **Sweet Onion**, chopped
3 cups **Chinese Cabbage**, finely chopped
3 cloves **Garlic**, minced
4 tablespoons **Grape Seed Oil** or **Olive Oil**
2 tablespoons **Sesame Oil**
¼ cup or less good quality **Teriyaki Sauce**
Garlic Salt & **Pepper**

Cook brown rice following directions on label and put aside.

In 4 tablespoons of grape seed oil or olive oil, sauté all of the cabbage, garlic and onions. (If you want to add other veggies or meat, this would be the time.) Now add rice and continue sautéing. Finally, add sesame oil, teriyaki sauce, garlic salt, and pepper.

Examples of veggies and meat to add: bell pepper, broccoli, green onions, mushrooms, chicken, steak, shrimp... use your imagination!

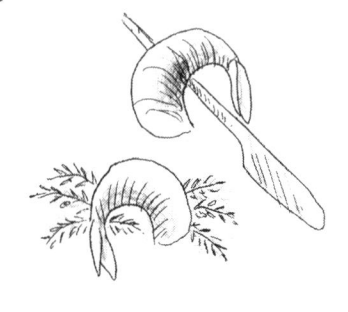

Stir Fried Brown Rice

4 cups **Brown Rice**, cooked
2 tablespoons **Olive Oil**
2 tablespoons **Butter**
¼ pound **Snow Peas**
3 cups thinly sliced **Bok Choy** stems and leaves
4 ounces fresh **Shitake Mushrooms**, stems removed and sliced
1 whole **Sweet Onion**
1/2 cup **Green Onions**, chopped
1 ½ tablespoons **Asian Sesame Oil**
2 tablespoons low sodium **Soy Sauce**

Follow directions for 4 cups of brown rice. You can use quick brown rice if you don't have a rice maker.

In a wok or pan, sauté veggies in butter and olive oil. Add cooked brown rice and sauté all together until veggies are done but still crispy. Next add the sesame oil and soy sauce. Serve with meat, chicken or fish.

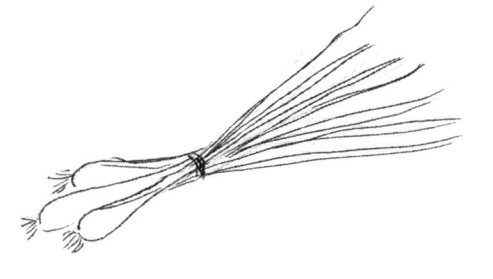

My Recipes...

My Recipes...

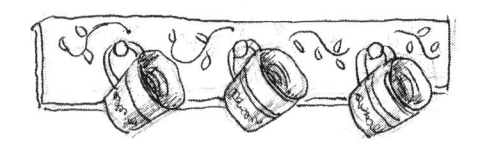

Sweets

Almond Cornmeal Shortcakes with Strawberries...... 142
Chocolate Carmel Corn 144
Chocolate Truffles 145
Crunchy Carmel Cashew Corn...................................... 146
Fresh Apple Sauce 147
Fudge Brownies.. 148
Healthy Apple Crisp 149
Healthy Maple Shortbread 150
Healthy Strawberry Topping 151
Hearty, Delicious Pumpkin Cookies 152
Homemade Graham Crackers 153
Homemade Marshmallows.. 155
No-Bake Strawberry Cheesecake.................................. 157
Pumpkin Fudge 158
Pumpkin Maple Cheesecake 159
Pumpkin Mousse Pie.. 160
Quick Fudge 161
Strawberry & Whipped Cream Parfait........................ 162
Whipped Cream.. 162
Whole Wheat Chocolate Chip Cookies 163
5-minute Strawberry Tortilla Pie 164

Almond Cornmeal Shortcakes with Strawberries

SHORTCAKES:
¾ cup Sliced Almonds
¾ cup Maple Sugar, or organic White Sugar
6 tablespoons Butter, room temperature, plus more for tins
2 large Eggs
1 teaspoon Vanilla Extract
¼ teaspoon Salt
½ cup Flour, ¼ cup Oat Flour, ¼ cup Whole Wheat Pastry Flour, spooned and leveled, plus more for tins
½ cup Yellow Cornmeal

Preheat oven to 350°.

Butter and flour 6 jumbo muffin tins (each 1-cup capacity); set aside.

In a food processor or mixer, blend ½ cup sliced almonds with sugar until finely ground. Add butter, eggs, vanilla, and salt; process until combined, scraping down sides of bowl as necessary (mixture may appear curdled at this point). Add flour and cornmeal; pulse just until moistened.

Continued....

Almond Cornmeal Shortcakes with Strawberries (cont.)

Divide batter evenly among prepared muffin tins; sprinkle with remaining ¾ cup sliced almonds. Bake until golden and a toothpick inserted in centers comes out clean, 20 to 25 minutes. Cool cakes 5 minutes in pan; remove from pan, and transfer to a rack to cool completely.

FILLING:
1 pound **Strawberries**
1/3 cup plus 1 tablespoon organic **Sugar**
¾ cup **Heavy Cream**

Hull and quarter strawberries. In a medium bowl, combine with 1/3 cup sugar. Let stand until syrupy, tossing occasionally, at least 20 minutes (and up to 6 hours, covered and refrigerated).

In another medium bowl, using an electric mixer, whip cream with remaining 1 tablespoon sugar until soft peaks form. With a serrated knife, split cooled shortcakes horizontally. Place bottom halves on serving plates. Dividing evenly, layer with sweetened strawberries and whipped cream; cover with shortcake top, and eat with friends.

Chocolate Caramel Corn

20 cups popped Popcorn
1 1/3 cups Brown Sugar or Maple Sugar
1 cup and ½ cup Butter, divided
2 1/3 cups Light Corn Syrup, divided
1 teaspoon Vanilla Extract
4 cups Milk Chocolate Chips

Preheat oven to 250°. Coat a large roasting pan with cooking spray. Place the popcorn in the roasting pan and keep warm in the oven.

In a heavy saucepan over medium heat, combine brown sugar, 1 cup butter and 1/3 cup corn syrup. Heat, without stirring, to 250° - 265° on candy thermometer or until a small amount of syrup dropped into cold water forms a rigid ball. Remove from heat and stir in vanilla.

Pour syrup over popcorn and stir to coat. Return popcorn to oven. In the same saucepan, combine chocolate chips with remaining ½ cup butter and 2 cups corn syrup. Cook, stirring, over medium heat, until chocolate is melted. Remove from heat and quickly pour over popcorn, stirring to coat.

Return popcorn to oven for 30 to 40 minutes, stirring occasionally. Remove and pour out onto waxed paper lined baking sheets to cool completely.

Chocolate Truffles

Basic truffle ingredients:

> 8 ounces of **Semi-sweet** or **Bittersweet Chocolate** (quality—62% cacao or higher), well chopped into small pieces or **Chocolate Chips**
>
> ½ cup **Heavy Cream**
>
> 1 teaspoon **Vanilla Extract**

Truffle coatings:
  Cocoa Powder
  Walnuts, finely chopped
  Almonds, finely chopped

In a small, heavy saucepan bring the cream to a simmer over medium heat (this may take a while, be sure to stir and scrape down the sides with a rubber spatula every few minutes).

Place the chocolate in a separate bowl. Pour the cream over the chocolate, add the vanilla, and allow to stand for a few minutes then stir until smooth. (This chocolate base is called ganache.)

Allow to cool, then place in the refrigerator for two hours. Scoop a heaping teaspoon amount of the ganache, and quickly (as it will melt from the heat of your hands) hand-roll well-formed balls. Place on a baking sheet lined with parchment paper and store in the refrigerator overnight.

Roll in cocoa powder or chopped nuts and serve, or place back in the refrigerator until needed.

Makes 30-40 chocolate truffles.

Crunchy Caramel Cashew Corn

4 tablespoons **Butter**, plus more for baking sheet

10 cups salted **Popped Popcorn** (½ cup kernels or 3.3 ounce bag microwave popcorn. Use Newman's Own microwave popcorn; it's better for you.)

1 cup **Cashews** or any type of nuts you like, coarsely chopped.

½ cup **Light Brown Sugar**, packed

Salt to taste

Preheat oven to 300°. Butter a large rimmed baking sheet and set aside. Place popcorn in a large bowl. If using cashews add to bowl and toss to combine. Set aside. In a small saucepan, bring butter, sugar, ½ teaspoon salt and 2 tablespoons water to a boil, stirring constantly. Working quickly, drizzle popcorn with sugar syrup, and toss well.

Spread popcorn evenly on the prepared baking sheet. Bake tossing occasionally until golden and shiny, about 40 minutes. Transfer hot popcorn to wax paper lined baking sheet. Let cool and break up into pieces.

Fresh Apple Sauce

2 of your favorite **Apples**
3 shakes of **Cinnamon**
Sweetener to taste, such as **Stevia, Maple Syrup, Honey,** or **Sugar**
1 teaspoon of **Lemon Juice**

Peel apples and cut into slices. Place apples, cinnamon, sweetener and lemon into food processor, and process until apple is the desired texture.

This sauce should be eaten soon after it is made because it can turn a little brown, and the health benefit is best when used immediately.

Fudge Brownies

1 cup **Butter**, softened
6 1-ounce squares **Unsweetened Chocolate**
2½ cups **Sugar** (try Maple Sugar or Organic Cane Sugar)
1 teaspoon **Vanilla**
3 **Eggs**
1 cup **Oat Flour**
½ teaspoon **Salt**
1 cup chopped **Nuts**, your choice

In a saucepan over low heat, melt the butter and chocolate, making sure to stir the whole time. Combine the remaining ingredients in a bowl, then add the warm butter and chocolate and mix well. Pour the mixture into a 9 x 9 inch baking pan, and bake at 350° for 35 to 45 minutes. Don't overbake!

These brownies are really gooey and decadent.

Healthy Apple Crisp

6 to 8 **Tart Apples**, peeled and cubed
2 cups **Brown Sugar**
1 cup **Oat Flour**
½ cup **Flax Meal**
1 ½ cups **Whole Wheat Pastry Flour**
2 tablespoons **Cinnamon**
¾ cup **Salted Butter**

Place chopped apples in a 9 x 12 inch or larger baking dish that has been sprayed with olive oil. Sprinkle 1 tablespoon of cinnamon on top of apples and some of the brown sugar. In a large mixing bowl, combine softened butter with all dry ingredients. Use your hands and mix well; the mixture should feel crumbly. Sprinkle on top of apples and then shake a little cinnamon on top. Bake at 350° for approximately 30 to 40 minutes. Check the apples with a fork and look for them to be soft and slightly squishy.

Top with vanilla ice cream or whipped cream (page 160).

Healthy Maple Shortbread

1 cup **Unsalted Butter**, at room temperature
1½ cups firmly packed **Light Brown Sugar** or **Maple Sugar**
1 teaspoon **Vanilla**
2 cups sifted **Whole Wheat Pastry Flour**

Preheat oven to 350°.

Hand mix all ingredients in a large bowl. Spray a nice short bread pan or small pie plate with olive oil spray and pat dough into it in an even layer. Pierce the surface decoratively with the tines of a fork. Since the shortbread will become firm and crisp when it cools, before baking, score the top without cutting all the way through the dough so that it can be broken apart into serving pieces.

Bake in the upper third of the oven for about 20 to 30 minutes, or until the top is puffed and lightly browned.

Healthy Strawberry Topping

1 pint **Strawberries**, cleaned and stemmed
1/3 cup of **Maple Sugar** or **Maple Syrup**
1 teaspoon **Vanilla**

Cut about 1/3 of the strawberries in half. In a saucepan over medium high heat, combine strawberries, sugar or maple syrup (maple syrup will make this thinner) and vanilla.

Cook, stirring occasionally, until sauce thickens, about 5 minutes. Remove from heat. In a blender, purée about 1/3 of sauce, then mix back into remainder. Store in refrigerator.

Hearty, Delicious Pumpkin Cookies

2 cups Brown Sugar
1 cup Butter
2 Eggs
2½ cups Canned Pumpkin
2 teaspoons Vanilla
4 teaspoons Cinnamon
1 teaspoon Salt
2 teaspoons Baking Soda
1 teaspoon Nutmeg
3 teaspoons Baking Powder
3 cups Oat Flour
1 cup Whole Wheat Pastry Flour
2 cups Chocolate Chips (or more!)

Cream butter and sugar. Add rest of ingredients and mix well. Drop spoonfuls on a greased cookie sheet and bake at 350° for 8-10 minutes.

This cookie is very cake-like and does not spread out. After the cookies cool, you can store them in an air-tight container in the refrigerator for up to two weeks. You can freeze the cookie dough for up to six months.

Homemade Graham Crackers

1½ cups **Whole Wheat Pastry Flour**, plus more for working
1 cup **Whole Wheat Flour**
½ cup **Untoasted Wheat Germ**
½ teaspoon **Salt**
1 teaspoon **Baking Soda**
1 teaspoon **Ground Cinnamon**
1 cup **Unsalted Butter**, softened (2 sticks)
¾ cup **Light Brown Sugar**, packed
2 tablespoons quality **Honey**

Preheat oven to 350°. Whisk flours, wheat germ, salt, baking soda, and cinnamon in a medium bowl; set aside. Put all ingredients into mixer and mix well.

Turn out dough onto a floured surface, and divide into quarters. Roll out each piece between 2 sheets of floured parchment paper into rectangles a bit larger than 9 by 6 inches, about 1/8 inch thick. Using a fluted pastry wheel or a fork trip, the outside edges or each rectangle, and divide into three 6 by 3-inch rectangles. Pressing lightly so as not to cut all the way through, score each piece in half lengthwise and crosswise to form four 3 by 1½-inch crackers. Stack parchment and dough on a baking sheet and chill in freezer until firm, about 20 minutes.

Continued...

Homemade Graham Crackers (cont.)

Remove two sheets of dough from freezer. Pierce crackers using the tines of a fork. Transfer to large baking sheets lined with parchment paper. Bake, rotating halfway through, until dark golden brown, 8 to 9 minutes. Repeat with remaining dough. Let cool on sheet 5 minutes; transfer crackers to wire racks to cool completely. Makes 20.

Crackers can be stored in an airtight container at room temperature up to 3 days.

Homemade Marshmallows

3 packages **Unflavored Gelatin**
1 cup **Ice Cold Water**, divided
12 ounces **Granulated Sugar** (approximately 1½ cups)
1 cup **Light Corn Syrup**
¼ teaspoon **Salt**
1 teaspoon **Vanilla Extract**
¼ cup **Confectioners' Sugar**
¼ cup **Cornstarch**
Nonstick Cooking Spray

Place the gelatin into the bowl of a stand mixer along with ½ cup of the water. Have the whisk attachment standing by.

In a small saucepan, combine the remaining ½ cup water, granulated sugar, corn syrup and salt. Place over medium high heat, cover and allow to cook for 3 to 4 minutes. Uncover, clip a candy thermometer onto the side of the pan and continue to cook until the mixture reaches 240°, approximately 7 to 8 minutes.

Once the mixture reaches this temperature, immediately remove from the heat. Turn the mixer on low speed and, while running, slowly pour the sugar syrup down the side of the bowl into the gelatin mixture. Once you have added all of the syrup, increase the speed to high. Continue to whip until the mixture becomes very thick and is lukewarm, approximately 12 to 15 minutes. Add the vanilla during the last minute of whipping. While the mixture is whipping prepare the pans as follows.

Continued...

Homemade Marshmallows (cont.)

For regular marshmallows:

Combine the confectioners' sugar and cornstarch in a small bowl. Lightly spray a 13 x 9-inch metal baking pan with nonstick cooking spray. Add the sugar and cornstarch mixture and move around to completely coat the bottom and sides of the pan. Return the remaining mixture to the bowl for later use.

When ready, pour the mixture into the prepared pan, using a lightly oiled spatula for spreading evenly into the pan. Dust the top with enough of the remaining sugar and cornstarch mixture to lightly cover. Reserve the rest for later. Allow the marshmallows to sit uncovered for at least 4 hours and up to overnight.

Turn the marshmallows out onto a cutting board and cut into 1-inch squares using a pizza wheel dusted with the confectioners' sugar mixture. Once cut, lightly dust all sides of each marshmallow with the remaining mixture, using additional if necessary. Store in an airtight container for up to 3 weeks.

No-Bake Strawberry Cheesecake

3, 8-ounce blocks of **Cream Cheese**, left out to soften
¾ cup of **Heavy Cream**
1 teaspoon pure **Vanilla**
1 quart of fresh **Strawberries**, washed and sliced length wise
11 packets **Truvia (Stevia)** or ½ cup of **Sugar**
   (Taste to make sure it is sweet enough.)

In a mixer, blend cream cheese, vanilla and sweetener until smooth. Prepare Graham Cracker Crust (recipe below) and scoop in ½ of the blended mixture. (For low-calorie version, spray a pie dish with cooking spray.) Cover with a layer of fresh strawberries. Next, scoop the rest of the blended ingredients over the strawberries and cover with another layer of strawberries. Garnish with whipped cream and a whole strawberry.

For the most delicious **Strawberry Chocolate Cheesecake**, add ½ cup **Cocoa Powder** to the blended cream cheese and mix well.

Graham Cracker Crust:
2 cups **Graham Cracker Crumbs**
½ cup melted **Butter**
1/3 cup **Sugar** or **Maple Sugar**

Combine all ingredients, and press over bottom and up sides of 9-inch pie plate. Bake at 400° for 10 minutes.

Pumpkin Fudge

1 cup **Almonds**
3 cups **Maple or Brown Sugar**
1 cup **Unsalted Butter**
1 can (5 ounces) **Evaporated Milk**
½ cup **Canned Pumpkin**
1 teaspoon **Pumpkin Pie Spice**
2 cups **Butterscotch Chips**
1 jar (7 ounces) **Marshmallow Cream**
1 teaspoon **Vanilla Extract**

Preheat oven to 300°. Butter a 9 x 12 inch pan and set aside.

Arrange almonds on cookie sheet and place in oven to toast for about 10 minutes. Remove from oven and set aside. In a heavy saucepan, combine sugar, butter, milk, pumpkin and spice. Bring to a boil, stirring constantly. Boil over medium heat until mixture reaches 234° on a candy thermometer. Remove from heat. Stir in butterscotch chips and melt. Next, stir in marshmallow cream, almonds and vanilla. Mix until well blended.

Pour into prepared pan, spread evenly, and cool at room temperature. Cut into squares.

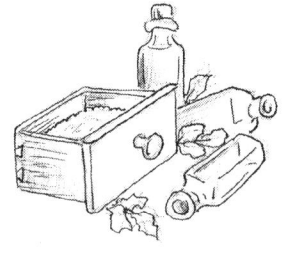

Pumpkin Maple Cheesecake

Graham Cracker Crust:
- 1 cup Graham Cracker Crumbs
- 3 tablespoons melted Butter

Mix butter and graham cracker crumbs and press against side of pie plate. Bake crust for just 10 minutes at 350°.

Pumpkin Maple Cheesecake Filling:
- 3 packages (8 ounces each) softened Cream Cheese
- 1 can (15 ounces) solid-pack Pumpkin Puree
- ½ cup pure Maple Syrup
- 3 large Eggs
- 2 tablespoons Cornstarch
- 2 teaspoons Pumpkin Pie Spice
- 1 teaspoon Vanilla Extract

Beat together all of the ingredients in a large bowl and then pour into the pie crust. Bake at 350° until center is just set, about 30 to 45 minutes. Let cool, cover and refrigerate.

Pumpkin Mousse Pie

Graham Cracker Crust:
    9 ounces **Graham Cracker Crumbs**
    ¼ cup **Sugar**
    ½ stick **Butter**

Pumpkin Mousse Filling:
    2 tablespoons **Unflavored Gelatin**
    3 large **Eggs**
    1 ½ cups **Canned Pumpkin Puree**
    ¼ teaspoon **Ground Allspice**
    ¼ teaspoon **Ground Ginger**
    ½ teaspoon **Salt**
    1 ½ cups **Heavy Whipping Cream**
    ¼ cups **Sour Cream**
    2 tablespoons **Powdered Sugar**
    ½ teaspoon **Pure Vanilla Extract**
    ¼ teaspoon **Ground Cinnamon**
    ¾ cup **Unsalted Butter**, melted

Mix butter, sugar and graham cracker crumbs in a bowl. Place the mixture in a glass pie dish that has been sprayed with olive oil. Press it evenly against the sides and bottom of the dish so that it forms a crust that is at least 1/8 inch thick. Place the crust in a 300° oven for 10 minutes then set it aside to cool.

Place 2 tablespoons of water in a small bowl then sprinkle the gelatin over the water. In large bowl, mix together the remaining ingredients. When they are completely whipped, add the gelatin. Spoon mousse filling into crust. Bake at 325° for 30 to 40 minutes or until set. Serve the pie cold with whipped cream.

Quick Fudge

1 cup of **Chocolate Chips**
¾ cup of **Mini Marshmallows**
1 teaspoon of **Butter**

Place all ingredients in a microwaveable mug or bowl and heat in microwave for approximately 1 minute. Stir fast and eat hot with a spoon, or pour into a waxed paper lined pan and let cool. You can make more fudge by doubling or tripling the recipe, Yum!

Strawberry & Whipped Cream Parfait

4 cups sliced fresh organic **Strawberries**
3 cups homemade **Whipped Cream**, sweetened with **Stevia** or other sugar-free sweetener

This recipe is too easy! Find a beautiful glass bowl and layer strawberries and whipped cream, all the way to the top. If you would like, add thin slices of pound cake or angel food cake, although that will make this a high-carb recipe. The strawberries and whipped cream are delicious without the cake!

Whipped Cream

1 Quart **Heavy Cream**
½ teaspoon **Pure Vanilla**
Sweetener, to taste (try Stevia for sugar substitute)

Place all ingredients in a blender or the bowl of a mixer. Blend on high. As soon as peaks form, your whipped cream is ready. If you over-whip the cream, it will turn into butter!

Whole Wheat Chocolate Chip Cookies

2½ cups **Whole Wheat Flour**
1 teaspoon **Baking Soda**
1 teaspoon **Salt**
1½ cups **Maple Sugar or Brown Sugar**
1 cup **Butter** (2 sticks) softened
1 teaspoon **Pure Vanilla Extract**
2 **Eggs**
2 cups **Semisweet Chocolate Morsels**

Put all of the ingredients together in a bowl and mix them carefully, but don't overmix.

Bake at 375° for 10 to 12 minutes until golden brown.

5-minute Strawberry Tortilla Pie

Preheat oven to 300° and place a large **Whole Wheat Tortilla** on a cookie sheet for ten minutes. You can also fry your tortilla in a pan in **Olive Oil** until crispy.

Cover cooled, crisp tortilla with fresh, washed, sliced **Strawberries**. Top with **Whipped Cream** and serve garnished with a whole **Strawberry**.

My Recipes...

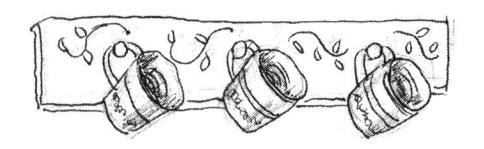

Beverages

Eggnog 168

Hot Spiced Apple Cider 169

Lemonade or Limeade Freeze 170

Not Your Usual Strawberry Smooothie 171

Eggnog

2 cups **Heavy Cream**
2 cups **Whole Milk**
1 12-ounce can **Evaporated Milk**
½ cup **Sugar** or **Maple Syrup**
¼ teaspoon **Ground Cinnamon**
1/8 teaspoon **Ground Nutmeg**
6 large **Eggs**
(Optional) ¼ cup **Brandy**
1 teaspoon **Pure Vanilla Extract**

Place milk, cream and evaporated milk in a large saucepan. Bring to a simmer over medium heat, making sure to stir. Combine sweetener, cinnamon, nutmeg, and eggs in a large bowl. Gradually add hot milk to egg mixture, stirring constantly with a whisk. Return the egg and milk mixture to the saucepan and cook over medium-low heat until thick, (about 8 minutes), stirring constantly. Pour into a bowl then stir in brandy and vanilla. Press plastic wrap onto the surface of the eggnog, and chill 8 hours or overnight.

Yield: 12 servings, ½ cup each.

Hot Spiced Apple Cider

½ cup **Real Maple Syrup**
2 **Cinnamon Sticks**, plus 6 sticks for serving
6 cups **Apple Cider**
6 whole **Allspice Berries**
1 **Orange Peel**, cut into pieces
1 **Lemon Peel**, cut into pieces

Pour the apple cider and maple syrup into a large stainless steel pot and heat. Cider should become very hot, but do not let it boil. Place the rest of the ingredients on a clean piece of cheese cloth and tie it closed. Add a string onto the bundle of spices and drop into the pot of very hot cider for 30 minutes. Take out the spice bundle and pour the cider into cute, pre-warmed mugs. Sprinkle with cinnamon and serve with a cinnamon stick.

10 Health Benefits of Cinnamon
http://www.healthdiaries.com/eatthis/10-health-benefits-of-cinnamon.html

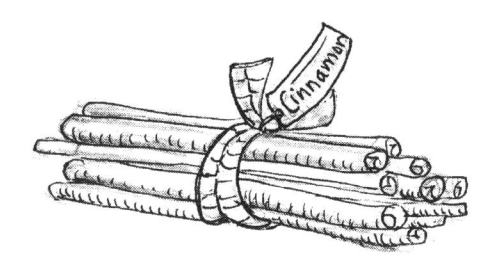

Lemonade or Limeade Freeze

¼ cup of fresh squeezed **Lemon** or **Lime** Juice
Stevia or **Sugar** to taste
Enough **Ice** to make it like an Icee

In blender, blend to desired consistency. Some people like it milder and some like it very sour.

Not your usual... Strawberry Smoothie

8 ounces fresh squeezed **Orange Juice**
10 **Strawberries**, stems removed
1 frozen **Banana**
¼ cup other **Berries**, (Blueberries and Raspberries)
1/8 cup **Yogurt** (optional)
Ice (to thicken it up)

Blend all ingredients in a blender. The best part of this recipe is that you can pour these ingredients into Popsicle trays and freeze or pour in plastic cups and freeze to make sorbet... Yum!

My Recipes...

My Recipes...

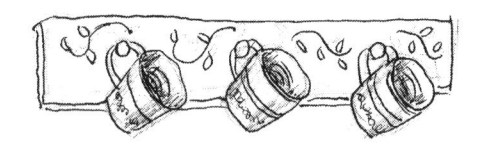

Index

Beverages, 167
Eggnog, 168
Hot Spiced Apple Cider, 169
Lemonade or Limeade Freeze, 170
Not Your Usual Strawberry Smoothie, 171

Breads, Crackers & More, 43
Ancient Grain Bread, 44
Farmhouse Crackers, 45
Flaxseed Crackers, 46
Focaccia Bread, 47
Healthy Pizza Dough, 48
Homemade Tortilla Chips, 49
How to Make Butter, 50
Ranch Bread, 51

Meats, 99
Autumn Farmhouse Stew, 100
Balsamic Skirt Steak, 101
Beef and Ale Stew with Dumplings, 102
Braised Short Ribs, 104
Cabbage Rolls, 105
Corned Beef, 107
Country-fried Steak, 108
Cowboy Stew, 109
Fried Wontons, 110
Health Benefits of Lamb, 111
Lamb Chops, 112
Lamb Kabobs, 113
Maple Pork Chops, 114
Pot Roast, 115

Pasta, Eggs & Cheese, 119
Dianne's Famous Quiche, 120
Eggplant Parmesan, 121
Mini Egg Muffins, 122
Ricotta Cheese, 123
Tomato Basil Pasta, 124
Tortilla Pie, 125

Poultry, 69
Braised Chicken in White Wine, 70
Chicken Parmesan, 71
Chicken Pesto, 72
Chicken Pot Pies, 73
Chicken Scallopini with Mushrooms, 74
Chicken Tarragon, 75
Cornish Game Hens, 76
Creamy Chicken Enchiladas, 77
Curry Chicken, 78
Delicious Italian Chicken, 79
Dianne's Famous 10-minute
    Baked Chicken, 80
Grilled Chicken and Garlic Pasta, 81
Mushroom Chicken & Rice with Wine, 82
Rosemary, Mushroom &
    Tomato Chicken, 83
Rosemary Turkey with Stuffing, 84
Salsa Lime Chicken, 85
Teriyaki Chicken Fingers, 86

Salads & Salad Dressings, 29
Cabbage Salad with Grilled Chicken, 30
Ceasar Salad, 31
Delicious Lemon Salad Dressing, 32
Flax Oil & Balsamic Salad Dressing, 33
Fresh Fruit Salad, 34
Oriental Cole Slaw, 35
Pasta Salad, 36
Potato Salad, 37
Shredded Tex-Mex Layered Salad &
    Creamy Lime Dressing, 38
Smokey Cabbage Slaw, Raw or Sautéed, 39
Strawberry & Spinach Salad
    with Chicken, 40

Index

Sandwiches, Empanadas & Wraps, 55
BBQ Tri-Tip Sandwich, 56
Best Tuna Sandwich, 57
Decadent Grilled Cheese
 Sandwich, 58
Empanadas—Meat or Veggie Pie, 59
Finger Sandwiches, 61
Incredible Egg Salad Sandwich, 61
South of the Border, 62
Steak Wrap, 63
The Ultimate Breakfast Burrito, 64
Tomato Basil Baguette Sandwich, 65
Turkey Peperoncini Sandwich, 66

Seafood, 89
Broiled Salmon, 90
California Sushi Roll, 91
Meals on a Grill, 93
Salmon Cakes, 94
Salmon Ceviche, 95
Salmon Tacos, 96

Side Dishes, 129
Delicious Pinto Beans, 130
Grilled Veggies, 131
Homemade Tortilla Chips & Salsa, 132
Homemade Mashed Potatoes, 133
Rosemary Baked Potatoes, 134
Sautéed Zucchini, Yellow Squash
 & Onions, 135
Stir Fry (Base), 136
Stir Fried Brown Rice, 137

Soups, 11
Asparagus Soup, 12
Blended Veggie Soup, 13
Cabbage and Mushroom Soup, 14
Country Cottage Clam Chowder, 15
Creamy Cauliflower Soup, 16
Garden Corn Chowder, 17
Hungarian Mushroom Soup, 18
Light Cheddar and Butternut Squash Soup, 19
Potato Soup, 20

Soups (cont.)
Real Jewish Chicken Noodle Soup, 21
Salmon Chowder, 22
Scallop Chowder, 23
Simple Mushroom Soup, 24
Split Pea Soup, 25
Tomato Basil Soup, 26

Sweets, 141
Almond Cornmeal Shortcakes with
 Strawberries, 142
Chocolate Caramel Corn, 144
Chocolate Truffles, 145
Crunchy Caramel Cashew Corn, 146
Fresh Apple Sauce, 147
Fudge Brownies, 148
Healthy Apple Crisp, 149
Healthy Maple Shortbread, 150
Healthy Strawberry Topping, 151
Hearty, Delicious Pumpkin
 Cookies, 152
Homemade Graham Crackers, 153
Homemade Marshmallows, 155
No-Bake Strawberry Cheesecake, 157
Pumpkin Fudge, 158
Pumpkin Maple Cheesecake, 159
Pumpkin Mousse Pie, 160
Quick Fudge, 161
Strawberry & Whipped Cream
 Parfait, 162
Whipped Cream, 162
Whole Wheat Chocolate Chip
 Cookies, 163
5-minute Strawberry Tortilla Pie, 164

Notes

Notes

Notes

Notes

Notes

Notes

The First Moms Club Press

No other books deliver such beautifully illustrated, much needed tools to teach anyone how to become an entrepreneur...

Dianne Linderman's series, *How To Become An Entrepreneurial Kid*, is a unique and beautifully crafted program that truly hits a nerve and fills a need by promoting financial literacy and entrepreneurial skills and attitudes for readers of many ages in a time when economic realities demand this kind of savvy and skill set at ever-earlier ages. "Everything in life starts with one idea!"

The series includes three enchanting, entrepreneurial storybooks and a business plan workbook for starting your own business. Beautifully illustrated by Delores Uselman Johnson, they are all educational and entertaining.

Perfect bind, 32 page storybooks, $8.95, and 20-page workbook, $5.95.

My Cookie Business

My Pony Ride Business

My Fishing Business

How to Become an Entrepreneurial Kid

4-Book package
$24.50

www.thefirstmomsclubpress.com • dianne@everythingthatmattersradio.com

The First Moms Club Press

A dynamic and inspiring series of How-to Books by Dianne Linderman

Illustrated by Delores Uselman Johnson

A most inspiring non-fiction story, *Everything That Matters in Life, Business, Parenting and Healthy Cooking*, 195 pages, $19.95

ISBN 978-1-456319-70-0

ISBN 978-1-935822-05-9

Everything That Matters in the Kitchen, a cook book with simple, healthy, delicious recipes in less than 20 minutes, 175 pages, $19.95

ISBN 978-1-935822-01-1

ISBN 978-1-935822-02-8

ISBN 978-1-935822-04-2

ISBN 978-1-935822-03-5

Everything That Matters in LIFE, BUSINESS, PARENTING & COOKING JOURNALS
Four 75-page Journals, $15.00 each

www.thefirstmomsclubpress.com • *dianne@everythingthatmattersradio.com*

The First Moms Club Press

For kids who love farm life and true stories...
the educational Animal Adventures workbook and DVD combine the author's love of animals and business.

ISBN 0-9704876-4-9

Fiona No No, a 32-page true story about a donkey diva, $8.95

ISBN 0-9764557-0-6

Animal Adventures at the Farm, an educational 58-page workbook, $8.95

978-1-935822-00-4

A fun, new family board game, *GASCAR Crazy Animal Races*

ISBN 0-9764557-1-4

A very first ☒ an educational animal DVD, *We Bring the Zoo to You*, $12.95

www.thefirstmomsclubpress.com • dianne@everythingthatmattersradio.com

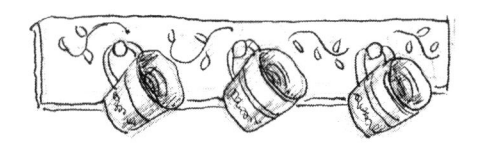

Made in the USA
San Bernardino, CA
04 April 2017